PUBLISHED FOR THE MALONE SOCIETY BY
MANCHESTER UNIVERSITY PRESS

Oxford Road, Manchester, M13 9NR, UK
and Room 400, 175 Fifth Avenue, New York, NY 10010, USA
www.manchesteruniversitypress.co.uk

Distributed exclusively in the USA by
Palgrave, 175 Fifth Avenue, New York,
NY 10010, USA

Distributed exclusively in Canada by
UBC Press, University of British Columbia, 2029 West Mall
Vancouver, BC, Canada V6T 1Z2

British Library Cataloguing-in-Publication Data
A catalogue record for this book is available from the British Library

Library of Congress Cataloging-in-Publication Data applied for

ISBN 978 0 7190 7711 1

First published 2007

Typeset and Printed in Europe by the Alden Group, Oxfordshire

THE FAMOUS VICTORIES
OF HENRY THE FIFTH
1598

THE MALONE SOCIETY
REPRINTS, VOL. 171
2006 (2007)

This edition of *The Famous Victories of Henry the Fifth* has been prepared by Chiaki Hanabusa and checked by John Jowett, G. R. Proudfoot, and H. R. Woudhuysen.

The Huntington copies of the 1598 Quarto and the title-page of the 1617 Quarto are reproduced by kind permission of The Huntington Library, San Marino, California. The Society is grateful to the British Library for permission to reproduce the title-page of its copy of the 1617 Quarto (C.34.l.9).

September 2006   JOHN JOWETT

INTRODUCTION

The Famous Victories of Henry the Fifth was entered in the Stationers' Register by Thomas Creede on 14 May 1594:

Thom̃s Creede. / . Entred for his copie vnder thand of m^r Cawood warden / a booke intituled / The famous victories of henrye the ffyft / conteyninge the honorable battell of Agincourt /

vj^d C^I

The first quarto of the play (STC 13072, hereafter Q1) was printed by Creede in 1598.[2] Only two copies are known to exist, one in the Bodleian Library (O) and the other in the Huntington Library (HN). The shelfmark of O is Mal. 232 (4), and that of HN is 12846. The present facsimile reproduces HN. This copy was once in the Kemble-Devonshire collection of English plays and playbills, which was purchased *en bloc* by Henry E. Huntington on 19 January 1914.[3]

---

[1] W. W. Greg, *A Bibliography of the English Printed Drama to the Restoration*, 4 vols. (London, 1939–59), i. 10. Edward Arber's transcription appears in *A Transcript of the Registers of the Company of Stationers of London*, 5 vols. (London and Birmingham, 1875–94), ii. 648. The capital 'C' which is written below the record of the sum paid in the right-hand margin signifies Upper Warden Gabriel Cawood, the licenser of the book (ii. 647). Greg transcribed a period after the 'C', which, according to Robin Myers, Archivist Emeritus of the Stationers' Company, does not look like an obvious full point in the original document (private correspondence). Arber did not reproduce it.

[2] Q1 is listed in Greg, *Bibliography*, i. 243–4 (no. 148 (a)). Among modern critical editions of *Famous Victories* are *Chief Pre-Shakespearean Dramas: A Selection of Plays Illustrating the History of the English Drama from Its Origin down to Shakespeare*, ed. Joseph Quincy Adams (London and Cambridge, Mass., 1924), pp. 667–90; William Wells, 'The Famous Victories of Henry the Fifth: A Critical Edition' (unpublished doctoral dissertation, Stanford University, 1935); Seymour M. Pitcher, *The Case for Shakespeare's Authorship of 'The Famous Victories' with the Complete Text of the Anonymous Play* (New York, 1961); *Narrative and Dramatic Sources of Shakespeare*, ed. Geoffrey Bullough, 8 vols. (London, 1957–75), iv. 299–343; and *The Oldcastle Controversy: 'Sir John Oldcastle, Part I' and 'The Famous Victories of Henry V'*, ed. Peter Corbin and Douglas Sedge (Manchester, 1991), pp. 145–99. Q1 is reproduced in facsimiles, in *The Famous Victories of Henry the Fifth: the Earliest Known Quarto, 1598*, ed. Charles Praetorius and P. A. Daniel (London, 1887) and *The Famous Victories of Henry the Fifth 1598*, ed. John S. Farmer, The Tudor Facsimile Texts (Edinburgh and London, 1912). Both facsimiles reproduced the Bodleian Library copy.

[3] For details of the collection and its sale, see Seymour de Ricci, *English Collectors of Books & Manuscripts (1530–1930) and their Marks of Ownership* (Cambridge, 1930), pp. 78–80, and Frank Herrmann, *Sotheby's: Portrait of an Auction House* (New York, 1980), pp. 124–6. Edmond Malone's autograph notes on the endpaper facing the title-page of O, where he refers to the play's performance in the 1580s and 1590s, are transcribed in Praetorius and Daniel, *Famous Victories*, p. v.

Q1 collates 4°: A–F⁴ G². The title-page is A1ʳ. The title, substantively the same as the Stationers' Register entry, is followed by an assignation to the Queen's Men.[4] Under these details is a printer's device representing Truth being scourged by a hand from the clouds. Creede's initials, 'T C', are between her feet. The motto reads 'VIRESSIT [i.e. VIRESCIT] VULNERE VERITAS' (The Truth regains strength by the wound).[5] Where the Stationers' Register identifies Creede as the copy-holder, the imprint below the device shows that he was also the printer. A1ᵛ is blank.[6] At the head of A2ʳ is an ornament,[7] which is followed by the head-title in roman type, 'The Famous Victories | of Henry the fifth, Conte ining the Hono-|rable Battell of Agin-court.'. Thereafter begins the text, which ends on G2ᵛ with the explicit 'F I N I S.'. The superfluous space below it is filled up by a tail-piece.[8]

The play is not divided into acts or scenes.[9] Many prose lines are set as though they were verse. What was presumably the end of a long first line of a prose speech in the copy is sometimes set as a run-over verse line (A2ʳ, TLN 25; A2ᵛ, 49; C1ᵛ, 538; C2ʳ, 563; G2ʳ, 1682), but this setting practice seems to be accidental, because it is not consistent throughout the text.[10] Each page normally has thirty-five text-lines. The normal count includes occasional blank lines placed at otherwise unmarked scene breaks; these, inserted before and in one case after stage directions, occur on D4ʳ (before TLN 1004), E2ʳ (before 1120), F1ʳ (before 1350), and G1ᵛ (before 1647 and after 1649). The blank lines probably resulted from unsuccessful

[4] The definite article before 'Queenes' (TLN 7) is spelled 'thc' instead of 'the'; the final letter is not a cracked 'e'.

[5] See no. 299 in Ronald B. McKerrow, *Printers' & Publishers' Devices in England & Scotland 1485–1640* (London, 1913), p. 117. See also Ornament 1 of Creede's ornament stock as compiled by Akihiro Yamada, in *Thomas Creede: Printer to Shakespeare and his Contemporaries* (Tokyo, 1994), pp. 60–1, 81.

[6] On the upper right-hand corner of A1ᵛ, O has a set-off showing a mirror image of a tiny part of the ornament on the facing page A2ʳ. This was probably caused by sheet A being folded before wet ink on this small part had dried. In HN, the show-through of part of the title-page is faintly visible on A1ᵛ.

[7] This is 'Orn 12' in Yamada, *Creede*, pp. 62, 82.

[8] See 'Tail-piece 96' in Henry R. Plomer, *English Printers' Ornaments* (London: [n.p.], 1924; New York:, [n.d.]), pp. 132, 219, and 'Orn 8' in Yamada, *Creede*, pp. 61–2, 82. According to Yamada, Creede used this ornament for the first time in three books printed in 1598.

[9] The play is, however, normally divided into twenty scenes in modern editions. Division of scenes 4–6 is slightly different among the editions by Praetorius and Daniel, Bullough, Pitcher, and Corbin and Sedge.

[10] Short second lines without indentation can be seen, for instance, in TLNs 40, 103, 307, 326, 334, 348, 360, 548, 560, 1016, 1721.

casting-off, and suggest that the text in sheets D–G may have been set by formes. Turn-overs were used presumably to preserve the lining of cast-off copy. Turn-downs appear on A3^r (TLN 105), A3^v (133, 136), A4^v (209), B1^v (257), B2^v (330), B4^r (439), B4^v (471), C3^r (665), C3^v (700), D3^v (951), and G2^r (1702); turn-ups occur on B3^r (TLN, 368), B4^r (434), D2^r (874), and D2^v (880). At TLN 136, the compositor turned down the text despite the large blank space left at 134. His use of an irregular turn-down here may perhaps reflect his need to waste space in relation to cast-off copy. A similar compositorial strategy may be observed at TLN 1270 where the compositor saved a line by turning-up a short stage direction. The frequent use of turn-overs in sheets A–D provides some basis on which to infer that these sheets were set by formes. It is, therefore, plausible that Q1 was set by formes throughout.[11]

The printer's measure is 80–82 millimetres in sheets A–F.[12] The variation seems to have been caused by paper shrinkage and uneven pressure from furniture. In sheet G the measure increases to 83–84 millimetres. One might ask whether the compositor widened the measure of his stick in order to set more type per line and so keep the final gathering to a half-sheet, but this appears not to be the case. If he had been seeking to save space he would have avoided wasting space by setting two blank lines on G1^v. The slightly longer line would perhaps indicate an interval between the setting of sheets A–F and G, and hence the use of a different or reset composing stick when work resumed on G.

The text is mainly set in black letter (textura) fount, with the use of pica roman type for stage directions, speech-prefixes, some proper names, and foreign languages (French, Italian, etc.).[13] Italic type is rarely used save for the title-page and an opening stage direction on A2^r.[14] Peter W. M. Blayney notes that pica black letter (20 lines measure 82 millimetres) was 'probably the most widely-used textura of its size in London' in the 1550s–1650s.[15] This particular black letter is remarkable for its square

<hr>

[11] There appear some contracted words, such as 'y^e' (e.g. B1^v, 248; C4^v, 744), 'thẽ' (e.g. B1^v, 273; B2^r, 284), 'watchmẽ' (B2^r, 284), 'cõfcience' (C2^v, 629), 'Pardõ' (C3^r, 646–7), 'thãks' (C3^v, 697), 'takẽ' (C4^r, 722), etc. All occur in full lines, which clearly shows the compositor making efforts to justify the line, avoid creating a new type-line or follow copy.

[12] On A1^r the measure is exceptionally wider (84 millimetres) in order to accommodate as many types as possible in the large-fount title.

[13] In the present Introduction, black letter and roman fount are both transcribed as roman.

[14] Elsewhere italic fount is used for Spanish on D4^v (TLN 1025). Upper-case italic 'C' is accidentally used for two speech-prefixes, 'Cobler.' (B1^r, 221) and 'Conft.' (E1^r, 1081), perhaps as a result of foul case.

[15] See his *The Texts of 'King Lear' and their Origins*, vol. 1, *Nicholas Okes and the First Quarto* (Cambridge, 1982), p. 502.

'T' in comparison with the round 'T' in other designs, and is of French origin.[16] Only the first three leaves of each sheet are signed, usually with black letter capitals and Arabic numerals. A1^r and G2^r are unsigned. B2^r is exceptional, being signed with a roman 'B', probably because the signature 'B2' is located between a roman stage direction and a roman catchword.[17] The setting of the catchwords is accurate.[18]

Collation of the two extant copies uncovered no press-variants resulting from stop-press correction. There are only two mechanical variants, both on D1^v:

TLN 821	belée ue,	O
	b eléeue,	HN
TLN 832	sayin gs,	O
	sayi ngs,	HN

The space in HN 'sayi ngs' is only slight. Both variant readings occur at the end of the line. This suggests that, when this page was printed, the pressure on the type from the right-hand margin was weak. As a result, types shifting to the right produced a space within a single word. This inference is supported by the fact that 'king' at the end of TLN 818 on D1^v reads 'ki ng' in both copies. The direction of the shifting of type suggests that the inner forme of sheet D (hereafter D(i)) of O was printed prior to that of HN.

There are a few other minor irregularities. In O, the impression of the catchword on B4^v looks imperfect, as is seen in Praetorius and Daniel's and Farmer's facsimiles. In the text as originally printed, a small sliver of paper peeled off from the surface and was folded to cover the catchword. The catchword under the folded paper reads 'Iohn.', as in HN. In Farmer's facsimile, the initial line on D3^v (TLN 946) appears to begin with 'atArchb.'. When this facsimile was published, O probably had a small hole

<hr>

[16] The type design is, most likely, identical with 'T 38' in H. D. L. Vervliet, *Sixteenth-Century Printing Types of the Low Countries* (Amsterdam, 1968), pp. 152–3. See also Frank Isaac, *English Printers' Types of the Sixteenth Century* (Oxford, 1936), Plate 54. In 1598 Creede used the same pica black letter in printing, for instance, the second edition of *A Looking-Glass for London and England* (STC 16680) and *The Honour of Chivalry* (STC 1804).

[17] In the same circumstances on F3^r, however, the compositor was careful enough to set up the signature in black letter.

[18] Minor typographical variations do exist, such as variant spellings of a word that follows, and the use of a period after the speech-prefix when it was set as catchword. To cite a few, 'Theefe' (catchword on B1^r) / 'Theef.' (the initial word on B1^v), 'Iohn.' (B4^v cw) / 'Iohn' (C1^r), and 'French.' (G2^r cw) / 'French King.' (G2^v). The longer word 'maintaine' (C1^v) is abbreviated 'main=' (C1^r cw).

before the speech-prefix 'Archb.' (now repaired) which made it possible to see part of 'What' in the first line on D2^v (TLN 876). In HN, there is a small hole or bump on 'h' of 'much' on C4^r (TLN 708). The impression appears to be irregular, but the reading on the verso page is not affected by it.

The headline, which first appears on A2^v, was set in large roman type, and reads 'The famous victories' on verso pages and 'of Henry the fifth.' on recto pages. There are no spelling variants. Typographical examination of the headlines reveals that only one set, comprising four running-titles, was used from sheets A to G throughout. This implies that one press was probably employed for printing the book. The arrangement of the four headlines by formes is as follows:[19]

Sheet	1^r	2^v	3^r	4^v	1^v	2^r	3^v	4^r
A	—	a	b	c	—	—	c	b
B	b	a	d	c	a	d	c	b
C	d	a	b	c	a	d	c	b
D	d	a	b	c	a	d	c	b
E	d	a	b	c	a	d	c	b
F	b	c	d	a	c	b	a	d
G	d	c			a	b		

The regular transfer between formes of 'd' and 'a' headlines on pages 1^r–2^v and 'b' and 'c' headlines on 3^r–4^v begins in sheet C and ends in E. This may indicate that the headlines were arranged by the same workman for the three sheets, and that the outer and inner formes of sheets C–E were printed consecutively. Rearrangement of the headlines in sheet F suggests that there may have been a break in the presswork between sheets E was F. In sheet G, the four headlines were divided between the two formes to speed up the process of imposition.

[19] Headline 'a' can be identified by the nick in the stem of the 't' in the '&' ligature. Headline 'b' has a broken upper terminal of the 't' in 'the'. Headline 'c' is remarkable for damage in the upper part of the stroke of the 'c' in the '&' ligature. Headline 'd' is characterized by its bent terminal of the 'y' in 'Henry'. George Walton Williams's identification of the headlines is not entirely accurate. In his 'The Good Quarto of *Romeo and Juliet*' (unpublished doctoral dissertation, University of Virginia, 1957), p. xx, read 'Headline II' for 'Headline IV', and *vice versa*.

Q1 is not without textual flaws. Misspellings are concentrated in three pages:

D1^r :   TLN 778 'summer' (? slumber), TLN 788 'stustice' (Iustice);
E2^v :   TLN 1170 'vncke' (vnckle), TLN 1138 'wronfull' (wrongfull);
E4 :   TLN 1260 'Carbuckles' (?).

This might suggest slips in the proofing. On B3^r a period is omitted (365) and a word is divided without a hyphen (366), both probably due to crowding. A speech-prefix, 'Hen.5.', is probably missing on A3^r (93), while another, 'Robin.', is wrongly repeated from the previous line on A4^r (159).[20] 'And And' on D2^v (877) is another compositorial repetition. With 'it it' on D3^v (976), the second 'it' is an error for 'if'. A stage direction is duplicated on D3^r (929, 933), and another direction, 'here he ſhakes her', is set as if part of a speech on D4^v (1035). All in all, the extent of printing-house error is unexceptional. Where two versions of the same joke are printed sequentially on B3^r at 374–9 and 380–5, the variants suggest that the passage was drafted twice in the copy.

In his analysis of compositors for eighteen editions of playbooks printed by Creede (including reprints) between 1594 and 1602, George Walton Williams identified two compositors, calling them Compositor A and Compositor B. They were distinguished on the grounds of the following compositorial habits: Compositor A regularly distinguishes proper names in stage directions by setting contrasting type, but B is indifferent to that practice; A prefers such spellings as *here*, *bene*, *-ee* and *-ie* endings, and the adverbial termination *-ly*, while B favours *heere*, *beene*, *-e*, and *-lie*, but is indifferent to *-ie*; A sets only the speech-prefix as catchword when the next page begins with it, but B sets the speech-prefix plus the opening word in the catchword position. Compositor A appears to prefer *do* and *ile* to *doe/doo* and *Ile*. Since Compositor B started to work for Creede only in 1598, Williams identified Compositor A as Creede himself, and B as his apprentice.[21] Thomas L. Berger identified Compositor A as the sole compositor in the 1600 quarto of William Shakespeare's *Henry V*, and added to the list of A's consistent spellings, *go*, *blood*, *O*, *me*, and *be*.[22] Akihiro Yamada also identified two compositors on the basis of his research on twenty-six playbooks printed by Creede between 1594 and 1602. He refined on A and

[20] This speech was probably spoken by 'Cobler'. See Corbin and Sedge, *Oldcastle Controversy*, p. 153.
[21] Williams, 'The Good Quarto', pp. 12, 35–7, 88; Paul L. Cantrell and George Walton Williams, 'The Printing of the Second Quarto of *Romeo and Juliet* (1599)', *Studies in Bibliography*, 9 (1957), 107–28, pp. 112–13.
[22] Thomas L. Berger, 'The Printing of *Henry V*, Q1', *The Library*, 6th series, 1 (1979), 114–25, pp. 114–15.

B's typographical habits, arguing that A typically inserts no space after a comma in verse lines but provides a wide space after a speech-prefix, while B generally introduces a space after a comma and sets either a wide or narrow space after a speech-prefix.[23] On the basis of these distinguishing marks of Creede's two compositors, both Williams and Yamada reached the conclusion that Q1 was set by Compositor A alone.[24]

My fresh examination of compositor identification yields the following observations. In the first place, internal commas and the word that follows them in short (unjustified) lines are normally unspaced (e.g. A2[r], TLN 33–4). Queries and colons after the final word in short lines are almost always spaced (e.g. A2[r], 18–9, 25; A2[v], 57). In addition to these, speech-prefixes in short lines are usually indented 3 millimetres from the left-hand margin (e.g. A2[v], 65–7, 69). Speech-prefixes and the period that follows them are set without a space (e.g. A2[r], 20–3). The text after that period is usually spaced to indent 2 millimetres (e.g. A2[r], 20–3). Finally, only the speech-prefix and not the first word of dialogue is set in the catchword position (e.g. catchword on A4[v], B1[r]). The typographical features represented by these coherent spacing and indenting habits offer 'psycho-mechanical' evidence that can scarcely reflect the influence of copy. It is widely accepted that, as the Elizabethan compositor could control minor typographical details with some degree of freedom, he could 'express his typographical personality despite the constraints his text laid upon him'.[25] Hence psychomechanical features provide the most secure basis on which to assert that only one compositor set the text of Q1.

A re-examination of spellings that elsewhere distinguish A from B, conducted with the use of the old-spelling electronic text in 'Literature Online', provided the following results (A's preference followed by B's, with the number of occurrences in Q1): *be* (128 A), *bee* (0 B); *bene* (11 A), *beene* (5 B); *blood* (8 A), *bloud* (0 B); *do* (45 A), *doe* (1 B), *doo* (9 B); *go* (55 A), *goe* (8 B); *here* (57 A), *heere* (2 B); *ile* (19 A), *Ile* (11 B); *me* (159 A), *mee* (0 B); *mony* (0 A), *money* (6 B); *yoong* (7 A), *yong* (10 A), *young* (5 B).[26]

[23] Yamada, *Creede*, pp. 192–4.
[24] Williams, 'The Good Quarto', pp. 32–3; Yamada, *Creede*, p. 192.
[25] See T. H. Howard-Hill, 'The Compositors of Shakespeare's Folio Comedies', *Studies in Bibliography*, 26 (1973), 61–106, p. 65, and his 'New Light on Compositor E of the Shakespeare First Folio', *The Library*, 6th series, 2 (1980), 156–78, pp. 163–4, respectively.
[26] The search was conducted by using 'Texts (Drama)' database in the Complete Literature Online (http://lion.chadwyck.co.uk/) on 6 April 2006. It included not only a simple keyword search but a wild-card search using the truncation symbol '*', with the result that the occurrences of such related words as *bloodie*, *herein*, *hereafter*, etc. were also included. The main text of this database omits the catchwords throughout. I carefully checked all catchwords myself in a facsimile text. The limited reliability of Literature Online is discussed by MacD. P. Jackson in '*Titus Andronicus* and Electronic Databases:

Though Q1's spelling *money* follows Compositor B's preference,[27] the weight of evidence, especially the occurences of the spellings *be, bene, blood, do, go, here, ile, me, yoong,* and *yong,* clearly signifies the presence of Compositor A. Taking all typographical and spelling evidence into account, the results cumulatively suggest that only one compositor set Q1 and that he was Compositor A, probably none other than Thomas Creede himself.

All sheets but G of both copies show watermarks. In sheets A–F, watermarks appear in the middle of the spine fold of conjugate leaves 1 and 4 or of leaves 2 and 3. The fact that no watermark is visible in leaves G1–2 of either copy suggests that the final sheet was probably printed by half-sheet imposition; the four pages in sheet G were probably imposed in one forme, printing both sides of paper, thereby producing two sets of the same half sheet.[28] Examination of the watermarks reveals that they are of at least three kinds: Pot, Hand, and Hand-and-Star. In quarto format, only a small part of the watermark design is visible in the gutter of the book, and in the two copies some marks were heavily impaired and some partly invisible to the extent that it is hard to identify them. Distribution of watermark designs is as follows:

O :   A: Pot; B: Hand & Star; C: H&S; D: H&S; E: H&S; F: Pot.

HN: A: H&S; B: Hand; C: H&S; D: H&S; E: H&S; F: Pot.[29]

Since the three designs represent favourite marks in 'Normandy and other parts of northern and central France', they suggest that O and HN were printed on a mixed stock of French paper.[30]

*

A Correction and a Warning', *Notes and Queries*, 244 (1999), 209–10, and in his *Defining Shakespeare: 'Pericles' as Test Case* (Oxford, 2003), pp. 196–7.

[27] Compositor A may have departed from his spelling preference due to the influence of copy.

[28] It is hard to make a conclusive argument about half-sheet imposition in sheet G based only on the watermarks of the two extant copies. It may, however, have been the most appropriate method for Creede in terms of speed and efficiency. For half-sheet imposition, see Philip Gaskell, *A New Introduction to Bibliography* (Oxford, 1974), pp. 83, 106, figs. 48–9.

[29] O sheets D and E have a somewhat deformed mark which looks identical with that of HN sheet D. The watermarks in O sheet F and HN sheet F are similar. Standard references consulted include C. M. Briquet, *Les filigranes: dictionnaire historique des marques du papier dès leur apparition vers 1282 jusqu'en 1600*, 4 vols. (Geneva, 1907; repr. New York, 1966); W. A. Churchill, *Watermarks in Paper in Holland, England, France, etc., in the XVII and XVIII Centuries and their Interconnection* (Amsterdam, 1935); Edward Heawood, *Watermarks Mainly of the 17th and 18th Centuries* (Hilversum, 1950); and *Likhachev's Watermarks: An English-Language Version*, ed. J. S. G. Simmons *et al.*, 2 vols. (Amsterdam, 1994).

[30] See Heawood, *Watermarks*, pp. 24, 26. O sheet B and HN sheet E may have the common mark which is also detected in sheet B of the Huntington copy of *James IV* (STC 12308) printed by Creede in 1598. The watermark in HN sheet A appears in sheet G of the Huntington copy of the second edition of *Looking-Glass*, also printed by Creede in 1598.

Creede, who was made free of the Stationers' Company on 7 October 1578 by Thomas East, started his business in London in 1593.[31] By the time he finished his career in 1617, he had printed 386 items listed in the revised *STC*, comprising 294 works. Literary works form 38.4 per cent (113 works), and religious books constitute 38.1 per cent (112 works) of the output of his shop.[32] Q1 is one of forty-four editions of thirty-five different plays Creede printed throughout his career. Of those plays, twenty-nine were first editions of new plays.[33] This means that, of 241 first editions of plays printed while he was active as one of twenty-odd master printers (1593–1617), 12 per cent were issued from his printing-house.[34] His printed dramatic works include Shakespeare's *The First Part of the Contention* (1594, STC 26099), *Romeo and Juliet* (1599, STC 22323), *Henry V* (1600, STC 22289), and *The Merry Wives of Windsor* (1602, STC 22299), also Robert Greene's *Alphonsus, King of Aragon* (1599, STC 12233), John Marston's *Jack Drum's Entertainment* (1601, STC 7423), Thomas Dekker's *The Magnificent Entertainment* (1604, STC 6510), and George Chapman's *Monsieur d'Olive* (1606, STC 4983).

The year 1598, when Q1 was printed, was the third busiest of Creede's career. Yamada's statistics reveal that in 1598 he printed 369.5 edition sheets, that is, 9.85 quarto pages a day on the basis of 300 working days in a year.[35] He issued fourteen items in 1598, of which he printed

[31] Arber, *Transcript*, ii. 679. Yamada infers, in *Creede*, p. 3, that he was probably born in 1554, as an apprentice could not be allowed, unless by patrimony, to become a freeman before the age of twenty-four. His printing-house was opened 'at the sign of the Catherine Wheel near the Old Swan in Thames Street', a few hundred yards west of London Bridge. The first books he issued there were reprints of Robert Greene's *Gwydonius* (STC 12263) and *Mamillia* (STC 12270), the latter printed for William Ponsonby.

[32] During the first twelve years (1593–1604), his main interest was in the publication of literary works. After 1605, his business shifted to religious books until 1613 (Yamada, *Creede*, pp. 24, 159–61).

[33] See Yamada, *Creede*, pp. 241–3, and his 'Thomas Creede', in *Dictionary of Literary Biography: The British Literary Book Trade, 1475–1700*, ed. J. K. Bracken and J. Silver, 170 (Detroit, 1996), 65–70, p. 70. Adrian Weiss, in his review of *Creede*, in *Analytical and Enumerative Bibliography*, 9 (1995), 61–8, p. 64, on the basis of newly discovered shared printing, increased the total output by 29.5 sheets, which include sheets from two editions of Thomas Dekker and Thomas Middleton's *1 Honest Whore* (STC 6501 and 6501.5). Details of Creede's biography, business transactions, and connections with his fellow printers and publishers as discussed below are largely from Yamada's work; and *A Dictionary of Printers and Booksellers in England, Scotland and Ireland, and of Foreign Printers of English Books 1557–1640*, ed. Ronald B. McKerrow (London, 1910), pp. 80–1.

[34] For the number of first editions published during that time, see Greg, nos. 112–352 in his *Bibliography*, i. 191–ii. 494.

[35] By Yamada's figures (*Creede*, p. 38), revised in the light of Weiss's findings, the maximum annual production rate of Creede's printing-house was in 1606, when he printed 386 edition sheets.

seven, including Q1 and *James IV*, for himself, the second edition of *Looking-Glass* for William Barley, *Mother Bombie* (STC 17085) for Cuthbert Burby, and the second edition of *Richard III* (STC 22315) for Andrew Wise.[36] There is no evidence that Creede had more than one press, but Yamada accepted the possibility that he had a spare press 'partly because of frequent and unexpected mechanical trouble with the main press and partly because of the practical utility of a second press'.[37] By the summer 1595, he had two apprentices in his printing-house, John Wilkinson and Henry Vawse.[38] This was an offence against the Star Chamber Decree of 1586 which allowed a yeoman printer only one apprentice.[39] As a result, he was fined five shillings on 7 July 1595, but he seems to have been allowed to keep the two under the condition that he promise 'not to teach John Wilkynson the arte of pryntinge'.[40] Yamada surmised that Wilkinson and Vawse were able to work under their master until their apprenticeship expired in 1602.[41] When Q1 was printed in 1598, accordingly, Creede had at least one legally admitted apprentice and another workman in his printing-house, along with one main press and, probably, another as a spare.

In 1616, only three out of the seventeen books published by Creede were produced solely by him, while fourteen were printed jointly with Bernard Alsop, the printer of the second edition of *Famous Victories* (1617, hereafter Q2).[42] Creede started to take Alsop into partnership at this time, but their joint business was short-lived. They are known to have printed one book together (STC 4897), in 1617, and it was probably shortly after this that Creede retired from his business and Alsop succeeded to the tools of the older man's trade.[43] Creede's type and ornaments had already been in

---

[36] As to the nature of Creede's career as a master printer, Yamada argued that 'the general tendency during the first ten years, 1593–1602, was that he was concerned to print more books for himself than for others. [...] The general tendency, however, was reversed in the second decade, 1603–12: he printed more books for other booksellers' (*Creede*, p. 41). In 1598, 68.3 per cent of the total edition sheets, including Q1, were printed for himself (*Creede*, p. 38).

[37] Yamada, *Creede*, p. 42.

[38] Wilkinson became Creede's apprentice on 31 March 1594, and Vawse on 7 July 1595 (Arber, *Transcript*, ii. 195, 823).

[39] Arber, *Transcript*, ii. 812.

[40] Arber, *Transcript*, ii. 823.

[41] Yamada, *Creede*, p. 4.

[42] Alsop was freed by William White on 7 February 1610, according to D. F. McKenzie, *Stationers' Company Apprentices 1605–1640* (Charlottesville, 1961), p. 28.

[43] Yamada inferred that Alsop worked as a journeyman from 1610 onwards, that his involvement with Creede perhaps started from 1613, and that Creede probably died at the age of sixty-four in 1619 (*Creede*, pp. 10–11; 'Thomas Creede', p. 70). *STC* lists one item (STC 13428) in the printing of which Alsop independently had a hand in 1616 and

use for many years, but Alsop continued to employ them throughout his career.[44] Alsop must have acquired the one press that Creede had officially been allowed by the Court of the Stationers' Company on 9 May 1615.[45] If Creede had a second press, Alsop perhaps succeeded to that as well. In 1617 he may have been working two presses, as the use of two distinct sets of headlines for alternate formes and sheets in Q2 could suggest.[46] On 5 July 1623 Alsop and twenty other printers were ordered by the Court of the Stationers' Company not to 'erect any more presses hereafter but keepe themselues to the number that nowe they haue', and Alsop was allowed to have only one press.[47] This record suggests that he may have ceased to use the inferred second press at some time after 1617.

Of Creede's forty-four editions of thirty-five different plays, only Q1 and three editions of *Looking-Glass* (1594, 1598, 1602) were printed in black letter. Blayney argued that 'During the closing decades of the sixteenth century roman type displaced blackletter as the usual design for books of many kinds'.[48] Black letter continued to be used in such books as Bibles, law books, chronicles, proclamations, statutes, jest books, ballads, news pamphlets, and hornbooks, which either demand an appearance of anti-quarian dignity or serve as reading for the barely literate and learners of the alphabet. Presumably, Creede's choice of black letter acknowledged the popular character of *FV*. The contrasting use of roman in his edition of *James IV* (1598) may respond to Greene's intellectual status as 'Maister

seventeen items (including *Famous Victories* Q2) in 1617. See *A Short-Title Catalogue of Books Printed in England, Scotland, & Ireland and of English Books Printed Abroad 1475–1640*, ed. Alfred W. Pollard and G. R. Redgrave, 2nd edn., rev. by W. A. Jackson, F. S. Ferguson, and Katharine F. Pantzer, 3 vols. (London, 1976–91), iii. 5.

[44] Henry R. Plomer claimed that 'Consequently his later books are very poor specimens of typography, and his news-sheets were printed in the roughest possible manner', in his *A Dictionary of the Booksellers and Printers who were at Work in England, Scotland and Ireland from 1641 to 1667* (London, 1968), p. 4. It may be noted in passing that the same black-letter fount Creede had used for Q1 in 1598 appears to have been used by Alsop for printing two items in 1617 (STC 15381 and 21603).

[45] See *Records of the Court of the Stationers' Company 1602 to 1640*, ed. William A. Jackson (London, 1957), p. 75. Creede's use of two presses in 1598 would not be completely denied by this order, for, as Blayney put it in his *Texts of 'King Lear'*, p. 41, 'The reason why the Company rules were so easy to break and so difficult to enforce was probably that most printers kept at least one extra press in sufficiently operative condition to be used for proofing as a matter of course'.

[46] One set was used for A(o), sheet B, D(o), and sheet E. It was broken up at the final stage of printing, and two each of the four headlines were distributed in G(o) and G(i). The other set was employed in A(i), sheet C, D(i), and sheet F.

[47] Jackson, *Records*, p. 158.

[48] Peter W. M. Blayney, 'The Publication of Playbooks' in *A New History of Early English Drama*, ed. John D. Cox and David Scott Kastan (New York, 1997), 383–422, p. 414.

THE
FAMOVS VIC-
TORIES OF HENRY
The fifth:

CONTAINING
the Honourable Battell of
AGIN-COVRT.

As it was Acted by the Kinges Maiesties
Seruants.

LONDON
Imprinted by *Barnard Alsop*, dwelling
in Garter place in Barbican.
1617.

PLATE 1: TITLE-PAGE, Q2a (1617), BRITISH LIBRARY COPY (C.34.l.9)

THE FAMOVS VIC-
TORIES OF HENRY
The fifth.

CONTAINING
the Honourable Battell of
AGIN-COVRT.

As it was Acted by the Kinges Maiesties
Seruants.

LONDON,
Imprinted by *Barnard Alsop*, and are to be sold by
Tymothie Barlow, at his shop in Paules Church-
yard, at the Signe of the Bull-head.
1 6 1 7.

PLATE 2: TITLE-PAGE, Q2b (1617), HUNTINGTON LIBRARY COPY (61389)

of Arts'. It is impossible to determine whether Creede deliberately chose black letter for Q1 because it dealt with English history in contrast with the play on Scottish history, or whether black letter happened to be unavailable when *James IV* was printed.

*

The second quarto of *The Famous Victories* was printed page-for-page from Q1 by Alsop. It is more than likely that by 1617 Alsop found black letter old-fashioned, because he printed both Q2 and the fifth edition of *Looking-Glass*, printed also in 1617, in roman type. The title reads, '*THE | FAMOVS VIC-|TORIES OF HENRY | The fifth. | CONTAIN-ING | the Honourable Battell of | AGIN = COVRT. | As it was Acted by the Kinges Maiefties Seruants.*'.[49] Variant readings between Q1 and Q2 are numerous. According to William Wells, Q2 'reprinted the play with a few corrections and many new errors'. Some 1260-odd variations, appearing in nearly every line of every page, range from spelling, punctuation, and fount, to capitalization, line-division, and hyphenation.[50] Q2 exists in two issues, Q2a (STC 13073) and Q2b (STC 13074), both collating 4°: A–F⁴ G², distinguished from each other by a partly reset title-page introducing a variant imprint.[51] Five copies of Q2a and three of Q2b are extant.[52]

Both issues of Q2 name '*the Kinges Maiefties Seruants.*' as the acting company, instead of the '*Queenes Maiefties Players.*' as in Q1. P. A. Daniel suspected that Alsop was responsible for the change, which was due to James I's accession, and he found it difficult to believe that the King's Men, 'now long in the possession of Shakespeare's *Henry IV and V*, would have retained this poor stuff in their repertoire.'[53] Roslyn Lander Knutson also questioned ownership by the King's Men, arguing that 'There is no evidence to suggest the migration of the playbook to Shakespeare's company by 1617.'[54] On the other hand, Andrew Gurr inferred that

[49] At the top of the title is a decorated logotype '*THE*', which looks similar to one of Creede's type ornaments ('Log' 1, Yamada, *Creede*, p. 84).

[50] Wells, '*Famous Victories*', p. vi. Wells has a list of Q1/Q2 variants in Appendix A.

[51] Greg, *Bibliography*, i. 244 (nos. 148 (*b*I) and (*b*II)).

[52] Copies of Q2a are known to survive in the British Library, Trinity College, Cambridge, Worcester College, Oxford, the Folger Shakespeare Library, and Harvard University Library. Copies of Q2b are held in the British Library, the Bodleian Library, and the Huntington Library. Greg originally listed a Folger copy of Q2b in his *Bibliography*, but later corrected this as a ghost (iv. 1708). Edmond Malone's autograph notes on an inserted endpaper of Q2b (Mal. 152(6)) state that 'this edition is in the possession of Dʳ Wright' who also owned a copy of Q1.

[53] Praetorius and Daniel, *Famous Victories*, p. v.

[54] Roslyn Lander Knutson, *The Repertory of Shakespeare's Company 1594–1613* (Fayetteville, AR, 1991), p. 212.

the Chamberlain's Men acquired *Famous Victories* by way of the Queen's Men players when the two companies were merged in 1594.[55]

*

Q1 gives the impression of a corrupt and curtailed play of poor quality. The play appears to fall into two sections at TLN 855–6, one corresponding roughly to Shakespeare's *1* and *2 Henry IV*, and the other to his *Henry V*. Hence scenes 1 to 6 of Q1 loosely correspond to *1 Henry IV*, scenes 7 to 9 (up to D2^r, TLN 855) to *2 Henry IV*, and scenes 9 to 20 to *Henry V*.[56] It has been proposed that Q1, much garbled and abridged, was memorially reconstructed by the Queen's Men players from two original full-length plays for provincial performance in an enforced tour during the plague years 1592–4 in London.[57] Laurie E. Maguire's comprehensive analysis of the 'bad quartos' provides the criteria by which most reliably to determine the nature of play texts alleged to be memorial reconstructions; these include internal repetitions, verbal formulae, external echoes, and metrically corrupt verse. Textual repetition occurs in B1^r (TLN 226–34) and B1^v–B2^r (278–86). Q1 describes Prince Henry with the formulaic epithet 'the young prince' (17 times), while such expressions appear in abundance as 'Why' (43 times), 'But' (30 times), the oath 'sounds' (18 times), and 'Gogs wounds' (15 times). In sum, the play's style is, according to Maguire, 'heavily formulaic, especially in comic scenes' and in its first half. Despite her more usual scepticism towards memorial reconstruction, she finally endorses the long-standing belief that the play shows 'signs of compression from two plays into one' and is 'Probably MR [memorial reconstruction], at least in the first half'.[58] Scott McMillin and Sally-Beth MacLean proposed a different 'reconstruction' theory in which the text printed in Q1 was transcribed from dictation, which was 'one way the company put together a new book when they divided into smaller units'.[59] Other scholarship on

[55] Andrew Gurr, *The Shakespeare Company, 1594–1642* (Cambridge, 2004), p. 25.

[56] René Weis, ed., *Henry IV, Part 2* (Oxford, 1997), pp. 23–4.

[57] See John Dover Wilson, 'The Origins and Development of Shakespeare's *Henry IV*', *The Library*, 4th series, 26 (1945), 2–16, p. 10. See also *The First Part of King Henry IV*, ed. A. R. Humphreys, The Arden Shakespeare (London, 1961), p. xxxvi. Among modern editors, Herbert and Judith Weil suppose, in their edition of *The First Part of King Henry IV* (Cambridge, 1997), p. 25, that the extant play may be an abridgement of a single, long play which covered the career of Henry V from his youth to his marriage.

[58] Laurie E. Maguire, *Shakespearean Suspect Texts: The 'Bad' Quartos and their Contexts* (Cambridge, 1996), pp. 250, 379, 252, respectively. *Famous Victories* is one of only four plays where she admits that there is a 'strong case' for memorial reconstruction among forty-one 'suspect texts' (pp. 324–5).

[59] Scott McMillin and Sally-Beth MacLean, *The Queen's Men and their Plays* (Cambridge, 1998), p. 119.

the provenance of the printer's copy supports the hypothesis that Q1 is a memorially reconstructed play that has been condensed from either two plays or a two-part play on the reigns of Henry IV and Henry V.[60]

*

The play, which 'may be the earliest of extant English history plays among the professional companies', has so far received relatively little attention in its own right.[61] It is more often than not referred to as a major source of Shakespeare's *1* and *2 Henry IV*, and *Henry V*. Though many historical details come from the shared source material in the English chronicles, the dramatic structure and the shared presence of material not in the chronicles suggest a more direct connection, and Geoffrey Bullough was confident that 'Shakespeare certainly recalled [*Famous Victories*] in shaping his threefold account of the hero-king'.[62] Recent editors of Shakespeare's 'Henry plays' have also agreed that *Famous Victories* served, directly or indirectly, as a source for the trilogy.[63]

The authorship of the play has long been open to question, and is likely to remain so. It has been variously attributed to Shakespeare, Richard Tarlton, Robert Greene, Samuel Rowley, and others, and is currently best regarded as anonymous.[64] The principal source is clearly not Holinshed's

[60] Giorgio Melchiori reaches the conclusion widely shared by current editors and critics of the play that Q1 is 'an extremely poorly-put-together memorial report of an old play, possibly in two parts', in his edition of *The Second Part of King Henry IV* (Cambridge, 1989), p. 8.

[61] McMillin and MacLean, *Queen's Men*, p. 89.

[62] Bullough, *Narrative*, iv. 159.

[63] As regards *1 Henry IV*, the Weils think it unlikely that *Famous Victories* can have been 'a direct source for much of *1 Henry IV* ', in their *First Part of King Henry IV*, p. 25. Conversely, David Bevington argues that 'Shakespeare knew and consulted a play very like *Famous Victories*', in his *Henry IV, Part 1* (Oxford, 1987), p. 18, and David Scott Kastan accepts the theory, mentioning *Famous Victories* as the essential source, in his *King Henry IV Part 1*, Arden 3 (London, 2002), p. 340. Detecting several echoes of *Famous Victories* towards the end of *Henry V*, Robert A. H. Smith speculates on inconclusive evidence that 'Creede's reader and/or his printers' employed by him added their recollections of *Famous Victories*, which they issued two years earlier, to the near-illegible manuscript of *Henry V*, or possibly turned for reference to a printed text of *Famous Victories* to identify readings where the manuscript was damaged, in his 'Thomas Creede, *Henry V* Q1, and *The Famous Victories of Henrie the Fifth*', *Review of English Studies*, NS, 49 (1998), 60–4, p. 64.

[64] See, for instance, [Shakespeare:] Pitcher, *The Case for Shakespeare's Authorship*, p. 3; [Tarlton:] F. G. Fleay, *A Biographical Chronicle of the English Drama 1559–1642*, 2 vols. (London, 1891), ii. 258–9; [Greene:] Philip Brockbank, 'Shakespeare: His Histories, English and Roman', in *English Drama to 1710*, ed. Christopher Ricks (London, 1987), 148–81, p. 150; [Rowley:] H. Dugdale Sykes, *The Authorship of 'The Taming of a Shrew,' 'The Famous Victories of Henry V' and the Additions to Marlowe's 'Faustus'* (London, 1920),

but Hall's *Chronicles* (1548). This is evident, for example, when Henry receives the embassage of the Archbishop of Bruges, where the stage direction reads, 'He deliuereth a Tunne of Tennis balles.' (D3ʳ, TLNs 929, 933), as is similarly recounted in Hall, 'a tunne of tennis balles', while Holinshed instead has 'a barrell of Paris balles'.[65] Bernard M. Ward pointed out that there is one instance of a phrase which is found in Holinshed but not in Hall, while Wells noted that several passages for which Hall does not supply the source have counterparts in John Stow's narrative, *The Chronicles of England* (1580).[66]

Confirmation of Q1's assignation of the play to the Queen's Men comes in an anecdote about the company's clown Tarlton claiming that he doubled the parts of Derick the clown and the Lord Chief Justice. *Tarlton's Jests* (1613, STC 23683.3) relates that, 'AT the Bull at Biſhopſ-gate was a play of *Henry* the fift, [. . .] becauſe he was abſent that ſhould take the blow: *Tarlton* himſelfe [. . .] tooke vpon him to play the ſame Iudge, beſides his owne part of the Clowne: and *Knell* then playing *Henry* the fift, hit *Tarlton* a ſound boxe indeed'.[67] '*Knell*' is said to be William Knell, another player of the Queen's Men. Since Knell was killed in June 1587, the play must have been performed by mid-1587 at the latest.[68] *Famous Victories* has a scene where Derick appears on stage along with the Justice, which makes Tarlton's doubling appear implausible, but some critics postulate that, to resolve a casting problem, the text could have been arranged for a particular performance so that Tarlton could double the two parts.[69]

pp. 3–22; [the Earl of Oxford:] Bernard M. Ward, '*The Famous Victories of Henry V*: Its Place in Elizabethan Dramatic Literature', *Review of English Studies*, 4 (1928), 270–94.

[65] *Hall's Chronicle*, printed for J. Johnson and others (London, 1809; repr. New York, 1965), p. 57; *Holinshed's Chronicles of England, Scotland, and Ireland*, printed for J. Johnson and others, 6 vols. (London, 1808; repr. New York, 1965), iii. 64. See Wells, '*Famous Victories*', p. ix, and *King Henry V*, ed. Andrew Gurr (Cambridge, 1992), p. 16, n. 2. It has been urged also that 'Kidcocks in Normandie' (E1ᵛ, 1106), Henry's first landing place in France, follows Hall's 'Kyd Caux', not Holinshed's 'Kidcaur' (Gurr, *King Henry V*, p. 227), but, as Proudfoot and Woudhuysen have privately pointed out, Holinshed clearly reads 'Kidcaux'.

[66] Ward, '*Famous Victories*', p. 279; Wells, '*Famous Victories*', p. xv. Wells provides comprehensive discussions of the sources of the play (pp. viii–xix).

[67] 'An excellent Ieſt of *Tarlton* ſuddenly ſpoken', ll. 1–7, on C2ᵛ. The original *Jests* comprises three parts, and the Second Part, where the reference appears, was entered in 1600 and assigned in 1609 (Arber, *Transcript*, iii. 168, 402). The 1609 edition once existed in Germany, but it was destroyed during the Second World War (*STC*, iii. 311).

[68] McMillin and MacLean, *Queen's Men*, pp. 89, 196; G. M. Pinciss, 'The Queen's Men, 1583–1592', *Theatre Survey*, 11 (1970), 50–65, p. 54.

[69] See Corbin and Sedge, *Oldcastle Controversy*, p. 27. Melchiori thought that 'the players may have altered the original to meet an emergency', in his *Second Part of King Henry IV*, p. 8, n. 3. Gurr likewise stated that 'the absence of any player from a performance would have called for some hasty adjustments, and Dericke's first comic scene

The Tarlton anecdote is widely accepted among recent critics, although a minority still insists that the doubling is unworkable.[70]

A play featuring Henry V was mentioned twice elsewhere prior to the appearance of Shakespeare's play. Thomas Nashe's *Pierce Penniless* (1592, STC 18371) refers to '*Henrie* the fifth represented on the Stage, leading the French King prisoner, and forcing both him and the Dolphin to sweare fealty'.[71] If Nashe was referring to *Famous Victories*, his memory was incorrect: it is the Duke of Burgundy who accompanies the Dauphin in swearing fealty. Philip Henslowe's 'Diary' records thirteen performances by the Admiral's Men of 'harey the v' from 28 November 1595 (with the enigmatic marking 'ne') to 15 July 1596.[72] Henslowe's inventory of the goods owned by the company as of March 1598 shows that 'Harey the fyftes dublet' and 'Harey the fyftes vellet gowne' were 'Gone and loste'. We also see 'j payer of hosse for the Dowlfen [Dauphin]' entered in the inventory of apparels of March 1598. In yet another 1598 inventory of apparel are listed 'Harye the v. velvet gowne' and 'Harye the v. satten dublet, layd with gowld lace'.[73] On the available evidence, it is quite unclear whether the 'Henry V' plays mentioned by Nashe and Henslowe were *Famous Victories* or some other lost version of the popular story. But, as David Bevington put it, Shakespeare 'certainly had the opportunity to

---

with the Justice might have been cut in favour of the ear-boxing scene', in his *King Henry V*, p. 227.

[70] McMillin and MacLean took the anecdote as valid evidence for Tarlton doubling in *Famous Victories*, in their *Queen's Men*, p. 90. Gurr accepts Tarlton's doubling in the play as a matter of fact in his *Playgoing in Shakespeare's London*, 3rd edn. (Cambridge, 2004), pp. 154–5, 157. On the other hand, Bullough contended that Tarlton 'cannot have been playing Dericke as well as the Justice, since both appear at once. Perhaps he played John Cobler' (*Narrative*, iv, 307). Maguire asserted that 'Doubling of these roles is not possible in the extant *FV* text', in her *Shakespearean Suspect Texts*, p. 252. The Tarlton anecdote, which was published some twenty-five years after his death, should be treated with some scepticism, for by that time he had become the kind of iconic figure to whom any such anecdote would easily be attached.

[71] *The Works of Thomas Nashe*, ed. Ronald B. McKerrow, 2nd edn., rev. by F. P. Wilson, 5 vols. (Oxford, 1958), i. 213.

[72] *Henslowe's Diary*, ed. R. A. Foakes, 2nd edn. (Cambridge, 2002), pp. 33–4, 36–7, 47–8. A range of interpretations of this marking has been suggested so far. There is good reason to believe that at least it does *not* signify a completely 'new' play, for a couple of plays are marked so twice. It may indicate either 'newly revised', 'newly licensed', or 'newly entered the repertoire'. For a comprehensive discussion of 'ne', see Diana Price, 'Henslowe's "ne" and "the tyeringe-howsse doore"', *Research Opportunities in Renaissance Drama*, 42 (2003), 62–78. Price suggests that, since Henslowe used 'n' for '2' elsewhere in his Diary, 'ne' stands for '"twice" or "double"' the usual entry fee in 'a pricing strategy used to promote certain performances' (p. 65).

[73] Foakes, *Henslowe's Diary*, pp. 317, 319, 323.

see some version of the Henry V story on the stage in 1595–6'.[74] Perhaps it was in order to capitalize on the popularity of *1 Henry IV* (entered on 25 February 1598 and published within the year) that Creede decided to print *Famous Victories* in 1598, four years after his entry of it in the Stationers' Register.*

[74] Bevington, *Henry IV, Part I*, p. 19. The lapse in time once led E. K. Chambers to suppose that a 1594 edition of the play existed and is now lost. See his *William Shakespeare: A Study of Facts and Problems*, 2 vols. (Oxford, 1930), i. 384. The play is, however, not the sole example of playbooks printed by Creede a few years after the entry; *James IV* was entered by Creede on the same day (14 May 1594) as *Famous Victories*, and also published in 1598. See Arber, *Transcript*, ii. 648; Greg, *Bibliography*, i. 244–5.

* Early stages of this research and travel to libraries were made possible by the Fukuhara-Kinen Research Fund, and the project was completed with Grants-in-Aid for Scientific Research of Japan Society of the Promotion of Science (No. 16520169). I am grateful to John Jowett, Richard Proudfoot, H. R. Woudhuysen, Akihiro Yamada, Stephen Tabor, Yasuo Tamaizumi, Robin Myers, Eugene Giddens, and Matthew M. Hanley for helping me with their specialist knowledge, technical advice, and helpful comments.

THE FAMOVS VIC-
tories of Henry the
fifth:

Containing the Honou-
rable Battell of Agin-court:

*As it was plaide by the Queenes Maiesties
Players.*

LONDON
Printed by Thomas Creede, 1598.

THE
FAMOVS VIC-
tories of Henry the
fifth:
Containing the Honou-
rable Battell of Agin-court.

As it was plaide by the Queenes Maiesties
Players.

LONDON
Printed by Thomas Creede, 1598.

The Famous Victories

of Henry the fifth, Conteining the Honorable Battell of Agin-court.

Enter the yoong Prince, Ned, and Tom.

Henry the fifth.

Come away Ned and Tom.
    Both. Here my Lord.
    Henr.5. Come away my Lads:
Tell me sirs, how much gold haue you got?
  Ned. Faith my Lord, I haue got fiue hundred pound.
  Hen.5. But tell me Tom, how much hast thou got?
  Tom. Faith my Lord, some foure hundred pound.
  Hen.5. Foure hundred pounds, brauely spoken Lads.
But tell me sirs, thinke you not that it was a villainous
    part of me to rob my fathers Receiuers?
  Ned. Why no my Lord, it was but a tricke of youth.
  Hen.5. Faith Ned thou sayest true.
But tell me sirs, whereabouts are we?
  Tom. My Lord, we are now about a mile off London.
  Hen.5. But sirs, I maruell that sir Iohn Old-castle
Comes not away: Sounds see where he comes.
           Enters Iockey.
How now Iockey, what newes with thee?
  Iockey. Faith my Lord, such newes as passeth,
For the Towne of Detfort is risen,
          A 2   With

With hue and crie after your man,
Which parted from vs the last night,
And has set vpon, and hath robd a poore Carrier.

   Hen.5. Sownes, the vilaine that was wont to spie
Out our booties.   40

   Iock. I my Lord, euen the very same.

   Hen.5. Now base minded rascal to rob a poore carrier,
Wel it skils not, ile saue the base vilaines life:
I, I may: but tel me Iockey, wherabout be the Receiuers?

   Ioc. Faith my Lord, they are hard by,
But the best is, we are a horse backe and they be a foote,
So we may escape them.

   Hen.5. Wel, I the vilaines come, let me alone with
      them.
But tel me Iockey, how much gots thou from the knaues?   50
For I am sure I got something, for one of the vilaines
So belamd me about the shoulders,
As I shal feele it this moneth.

   Iock. Faith my Lord, I haue got a hundred pound.

   Hen.5. A hundred pound, now brauely spoken Iockey:
But come sirs, laie al your money before me,
Now by heauen here is a braue shewe:
But as I am true Gentleman, I wil haue the halfe
Of this spent to night, but sirs take vp your bags,
Here comes the Receiuers, let me alone.   60

           Enters two Receiuers.

   One. Alas good fellow, what shal we do?
I dare neuer go home to the Court, for I shall be hangd.
But looke, here is the yong Prince, what shal we do?

   Hen.5. How now you vilaines, what are you?

   One Recei. Speake you to him.

   Other. No I pray, speake you to him.

   Hen.5. Why how now you rascals, why speak you not?

   One. Forsooth we be. Pray speake you to him.

   Hen.5. Sowns, vilains speak, or ile cut off your heads.   70
                                 Other.

Other. Forsooth he can tel the tale better then I.

One. Forsooth we be your fathers Receiuers.

Hen.5. Are you my fathers Receiuers?
Then I hope ye haue brought me some money.

One. Money, Alas sir we be robd.

Hen.5. Robd, how many were there of them?

One. Marry sir, there were foure of them :
And one of them had sir Iohn Old-Castles bay Hobbie,
And your blacke Nag.

Hen.5. Gogs wounds how like you this Iockey?
Blood you vilaines: my father robd of his money abroad,
And we robd in our stables.
But tell me, how many were of them?

One recei. If it please you, there were foure of them,
And there was one about the bignesse of you :
But I am sure I so belambd him about the shoulders,
That he wil feele it this month.

Hen.5. Gogs wounds you lamd them faierly,
So that they haue carried away your money.
But come sirs, what shall we do with the vilaines?

Both recei. I beseech your grace, be good to vs.

Ned. I pray you my Lord forgiue them this once.
Well stand vp and get you gone,
And looke that you speake not a word of it;
For if there be, sownes ile hang you and all your kin.
                                        Exit Purseuant.

Hen.5. Now sirs, how like you this?
Was not this brauely done?
For now the vilaines dare not speake a word of it,
I haue so feared them with words.
Now whither shall we goe?

All. Why my Lord, you know our old hostes
At Feuersham.

Hen.5. Our hostes at Feuersham, blood what shal we do
We haue a thousand pound about vs,   (there?
                    A 3   And

And we shall go to a pettie Ale-house.

No,no: you know the olde Tauerne in Eastcheape,

There is good wine: besides,there is a pretie wench

That can talke well,for I delight as much in their toongs,

As any part about them.

   All. We are readie to waite vpon your grace.

   Hen.5. Gogs wounds wait,we will go altogither,

We are all fellowes,I tell you sirs,and the king

My father were dead,we would be all kings,

Therefore come away.

    Ned. Gogs wounds,brauely spoken Harry.

      Enter Iohn Cobler,Robin Pewterer,Lawrence

             Costermonger.

Iohn Cob. All is well here,all is well maisters.

   Robin. How say you neighbour Iohn Cobler?

I thinke it best that my neighbour

Robin Pewterer went to Pudding lane end,

And we will watch here at Billinsgate ward.

How say you neighbour Robin,how like you this?

   Robin. Marry well neighbours:

I care not much if I goe to Pudding lanes end.

But neighbours,and you heare any adoe about me,

Make haste: and if I heare any ado about you,

I will come to you.

                        Exit Robin.

Law.Neighbor,what newes heare you of y young Prince:

Iohn. Marry neighbor, I heare say, he is a toward yong

For if he met any by the hie way,   (Prince,

He will not let to talke with him,

I dare not call him theefe, but sure he is one of these taking

                        (fellowes.

   Law. Indeed neighbour I heare say he is as liuely

A young Prince as euer was.

   Iohn. I,and I heare say,if he vse it long,

His father will cut him off from the Crowne:

                             But

110

120

130

140

But neighbour say nothing of that.

   Law. No, no, neighbour, I warrant you.

   Iohn. Neighbour, me thinkes you begin to sleepe,
If you will, we will sit down,
For I thinke it is about midnight.

   Law. Marry content neighbour, let vs sleepe.

        Enter Dericke rouing.

Dericke. Who, who there, who there?

                   Exit Dericke.

150

        Enter Robin.

   Robin. O neighbors, what meane you to sleepe,
And such ado in the streetes?

   Ambo. How now neighbor, whats the matter?

       Enter Dericke againe.

   Dericke. Who there, who there, who there?

   Cobler. Why what ailst thou? here is no horses.

   Dericke. O alas man, I am robd, who there, who there?

   Robin. Hold him neighbor Cobler.

   Robin. Why I see thou art a plaine Clowne.

160

   Dericke. Am I a Clowne, sownes maisters,
Do Clownes go in silke apparell?
I am sure all we gentlemen Clownes in Kent scant go so
Well: Sownes you know clownes very well:
Heare you, are you maister Constable, and you be speake?
For I will not take it at his hands.

   Iohn. Faith I am not maister Constable,
But I am one of his bad officers, for he is not here.

   Dericke. Is not maister Constable here?
Well it is no matter, ile haue the law at his hands.

170

   Iohn. Nay I pray you do not take the law of vs.

   Der. Well, you are one of his beastly officers,

   Iohn. I am one of his bad officers.

   Der. Why then I charge thee looke to him.

   Cobler. Nay but heare ye sir, you seeme to be an honest
Fellow, and we are poore men, and now tis night:

                     And

And we would be loth to haue any thing adw,
Therefore I pray thée put it vp.

  Der. First, thou saiest true, I am an honest fellow,
And a proper hansome fellow too,
And you séeme to be poore men, therfore I care not greatly,
Nay, I am quickly pacified:
But and you chance to spie the théefe,
I pray you late hold on him.

  Robin. Yes that we wil, I warrant you.

  Der. Tis a wonderfal thing to sée how glad the knaue
Is, now I haue forgiuen him.

  Iohn. Neighbors do ye looke about you?
How now, who's there?

Enter the Theefe.

  Theefe. Here is a good fellow, I pray you which is the
Way to the old Tauerne in Eastcheape?

  Der. Whoope hollo, now Gads Hill, knowest thou me?

  Theef. I know thée for an Asse.

  Der. And I know thée for a taking fellow,
Vpon Gads hill in Kent:
A bots light vpon ye.

  Theef. The whorson vilaine would be knockt.

  Der. Maisters, vilaine, and ye be men stand to him,
And take his weapon from him, let him not passe you.

  Iohn. My friend, what make you abroad now?
It is too late to walke now.

  Theef. It is not too late for true men to walke.

  Law. We know thée not to be a true man.

  Theef. Why what do you meane to do with me?
Sownes I am one of the kings liege people.

  Der. Heare you sir, are you one of the kings liege people?

  Theef. I marry am I sir, what say you to it?

  Der. Marry sir, I say you are one of the kings filching
Cob. Come, come, lets haue him away.   (people.

  Theef. Why what haue I done?

Robin.

180

190

200

210

Robin. Thou hast robd a poore fellow,
And taken away his goods from him.

Theefe. I neuer sawe him before.

Der. Maisters who comes here?

Enter the Vintners boy.

Boy. How now good man Cobler?

Cob. How now Robin, what makes thou abroad
At this time of night?

Boy. Marrie I haue béene at the Counter,
I can tell such newes as neuer you haue heard the like.

Cobler. What is that Robin, what is the matter?

Boy. Why this night about two houres ago, there came
the young Prince, and thrée or foure more of his companions, and called for wine good store, and then they sent for a
noyse of Musitians, and were very merry for the space of
an houre, then whether their Musicke liked them not, or
whether they had drunke too much Wine or no, I cannot
tell, but our pots flue against the wals, and then they drew
their swordes, and went into the stréete and fought, and
some tooke one part, & some tooke another, but for the space
of halfe an houre, there was such a bloodie fray as passeth,
and none coulde part them vntill such time as the Maior
and Sheriffe were sent for, and then at the last with much
adoo, they tooke them, and so the yong Prince was carried
to the Counter, and then about one houre after, there came
a Messenger from the Court in all haste from the King, for
my Lord Maior and the Sheriffe, but for what cause I
know not.

Cobler. Here is newes indéede Robert.

Law. Marry neighbour, this newes is strange indéede,
I thinke it best neighbour, to rid our hands of this fellowe
first.

Theefe. What meane you to doe with me?

Cobler. We mean to carry you to the prison, and there
to remaine till the Sessions day.

B   Theefe

Theef. Then I pray you let me go to the prison where
my maister is.

Cob. Nay thou must go to ye country prison, to newgate,
Therefore come away.

Theef. I prethie be good to me honest fellow.

Der. I marry will I, ile be verie charitable to thee,
For I will neuer leaue thee, til I see thee on the Gallowes.

Enter Henry the fourth, with the Earle of Exeter,
and the Lord of Oxford.

Oxf. And please your Maiestie, heere is my Lord Maior and the Sheriffe of London, to speak with your Maie-

K, Hen.4. Admit them to our presence.   (stie.

Enter the Maior and the Sheriffe.

Now my good Lord Maior of London,
The cause of my sending for you at this time, is to tel you
of a matter which I haue learned of my Councell: Herein
I vnderstand, that you haue committed my sonne to prison
without our leaue and license. What althogh he be a rude
youth, and likely to giue occasion, yet you might haue con-
sidered that he is a Prince, and my sonne, and not to be
halled to prison by euery subiect.

Maior. May it please your Maiestie to giue vs leaue to
tell our tale?

King Hen.4. Or else God forbid, otherwise you might
thinke me an vnequall Iudge, hauing more affection to
my sonne, then to any rightfull iudgement.

Maior. Then I do not doubt but we shal rather deserue
commendations at your Maiesties hands, the any anger.

K, Hen.4. Go too, say on.

Maior. Then if it please your Maiestie, this night betwixt two and three of the clocke in the morning, my Lord
the yong Prince with a very disordred companie, came to
the old Tauerne in Eastcheape, and whether it was that
their Musicke liked them not, or whether they were ouer-
come with wine, I know not, but they drew their swords,
                                                            and

and into the streete they went, and some tooke my Lord the
yong Princes part, and some tooke the other, but betwixt
them there was such a bloodie fray for the space of halfe an
houre, that neither watchmē nor any other could stay thē,
till my brother the Sheriffe of London & I were sent for,
and at the last with much adow we staied them, but it was
long first, which was a great disquieting to all your louing
subiects thereabouts: and then my good Lord, we knew not
whether your grace had sent them to trie vs, whether we
would doo iustice, or whether it were of their owne volun-
tarie will or not, we cannot tell : and therefore in such a
case we knew not what to do, but for our own safegard we
sent him to ward, where he wanteth nothing that is fit for
his grace, and your Maiesties sonne. And thus most humbly beseeching your Maiestie to thinke of our answere.

    Hen 4. Stand aside vntill we haue further deliberated
on your answere.

                              Exit Maior.

    Hen. 4. Ah Harry, Harry, now thrice accursed Harry,
That hath gotten a sonne, which with greefe
Will end his fathers dayes.
Oh my sonne, a Prince thou art, I a Prince indeed,
And to deserue imprisonment,
And well haue they done, and like faithfull subiects:
Discharge them and let them go.

    L.Exe. I beseech your Grace , be good to my Lord the
yong Prince.

    Hen.4. Nay, nay, tis no matter, let him alone.

    L.Oxf. Perchance the Maior and the Sheriffe haue
bene to precise in this matter.

    Hen.4. No: they haue done like faithfull subiects:
I will go my selfe to discharge them, and let them go.

                              Exit omnes.

Enter Lord chiefe Iustice, Clarke of the Office, Iayler,
      Iohn Cobler, Dericke, and the Theefe.

                B 2   Iudge.

Iudge. Iayler bring the prisoner to the barre.

Der. Heare you my Lord, I pray you bring the bar to
the prisoner.

Iudge. Hold thy hand vp at the barre.

Theefe. Here it is my Lord.

Iudge. Clearke of the Office, reade his inditement.

Cleark. What is thy name?

Theefe. My name was knowne before I came here,
And shall be when I am gone, I warrant you.

Iudge. I, I thinke so, but we will know it better before
thou go.

Der. Sownes and you do but send to the next Iaile,
We are sure to know his name,
For this is not the first prison he hath bene in, ile warrant

Clearke. What is thy name?   (you.

Theef. What néed you to aske, and haue it in writing.

Clearke. Is not thy name Cutbert Cutter?

Theefe. What the Diuell néed you ask, and know it so
well.

Cleark. Why then Cutbert Cutter, I indite thée by the
name of Cutbert Cutter, for robbing a poore carrier the 20
day of May last past, in the fourtéen yeare of the raigne of
our soueraigne Lord king Henry the fourth, for setting
vpon a poore Carrier vpon Gads hill in Kent, and hauing
beaten and wounded the said Carrier, and taken his goods
from him.

Der. Oh maisters stay there, nay lets neuer belie the
man, for he hath not beaten and wounded me also, but hée
hath beaten and wounded my packe, and hath taken the
great rase of Ginger, that bouncing Besse with the iolly
buttocks should haue had, that grécues me most.

Iudge. Well, what sayest thou, art thou guiltie, or not
guiltie?

Theefe. Not guiltie, my Lord.

Iudge. By whom wilt thou be tride?

Theefe.

Theefe. By my Lord the young Prince, or by my selfe
whether you will.

Enter the young Prince, with Ned and Tom.

Hen.5. Come away my lads, Gogs wounds ye villain,
what make you heere? I must goe about my businesse my
selfe, and you must stand loytering here.

Theefe. Why my Lord, they haue bound me, and will
not let me goe.

Hen.5. Haue they bound thee villain, why how now my
Lord?

Iudge. I am glad to see your grace in good health.

Hen.5. Why my Lord, this is my man,
Tis maruell you knew him not long before this,
I tell you he is a man of his hands.

Theefe. I Gogs wounds that I am, try me who dare.

Iudge. Your Grace shal finde small credit by acknow
ledging him to be your man.

Hen.5. Why my Lord, what hath he done? (Carrier.

Iud. And it please your Maiestie, he hath robbed a poore

Der. Heare you sir, marry it was one Dericke,
Goodman Hoblings man of Kent.

Hen.5. What wast you butten-breech?
Of my word my Lord, he did it but in iest.

Der. Heare you sir, is it your mans qualitie to rob folks
in iest? In faith, he shall be hangd in earnest.

Hen.5. Well my Lord, what do you meane to do with
my man?

Iudg. And please your grace, the law must passe on him,
According to iustice, then he must be executed.

Der. Heare you sir, I pray you, is it your mans quality
to rob folkes in iest? In faith he shall be hangd in iest.

Hen.5. Well my Lord, what meane you to do with my
man?

Iudg. And please your grace the law must passe on him,
According to iustice, then he must be executed.

B 3   Hen.

Hen. 5. Why then belike you meane to hang my man?

Iudge. I am sorie that it falles out so.

Hen. 5. Why my Lord, I pray ye who am I?

Iud. And please your Grace, you are my Lord the yong
Prince, our King that shall be after the decease of our soueraigne Lord, King Henry the fourth, whom God graunt
long to raigne.

Hen. 5. You say true my Lord:
And you will hang my man.

Iudge. And like your grace, I must néeds do iustice.

Hen. 5. Tell me my Lord, shall I haue my man?

Iudge. I cannot my Lord.

Hen. 5. But will you not let him go?

Iud. I am sorie that his case is so ill.

Hen. 5. Tush, case me no casings, shal I haue my man?

Iudge. I cannot, nor I may not my Lord.

Hen. 5. Nay, and I shal not say, then I am answered?

Iudge. No.

Hen. 5. No: then I will haue him.

He giueth him a boxe on the eare.

Ned. Gogs woundes my Lord, shal I cut off his head?

Hen. 5. No, I charge you draw not your swordes,
But get you hence, prouide a noyse of Musitians,
Away, be gone.

Exeunt the Theefe.

Iudge. Well my Lord, I am content to take it at your
hands.

Hen. 5. Nay and you be not, you shall haue more.

Iudge. Why I pray you my Lord, who am I?

Hen. 5. You, who knowes not you?
Why man, you are Lord chiefe Iustice of England.

Iudge. Your Grace hath said truth, therfore in striking
me in this place, you greatly abuse me, and not me onely,
but also your father: whose liuely person here in this place
I do represent. And therefore to teach you what prerogatiues

tiues meane, I commit you to the Fléete, vntill we haue
spoken with your father.

 Hen.5. Why then belike you meane to send me to the
Fléete?

 Iudge. I indéed, and therefore carry him away.
Exeunt Hen.5. with the Officers.

 Iudge. Iayler, carry the prisoner to Newgate againe,
vntil the next Sises.

 Iay. At your commandement my Lord; it shalbe done.
Enter Dericke and Iohn Cobler.

 Der. Sownds maisters, heres adœ,
When Princes must go to prison:
Why Iohn, didst euer sée the like?

 Iohn. O Dericke, trust me, I neuer saw the like. (ler,

 Der. Why Iohn thou maist sée what princes be in chol-
A Iudge a boxe on the eare, Ile tel thée Iohn, O Iohn,
I would not haue done it for twentie shillings.

 Iohn. No nor I, there had bene no way but one with
We should haue bene hangde. (vs,

 Der. Faith Iohn, Ile tel thée what, thou shalt be my
Lord chiefe Iustice, and thou shalt sit in the chaire,
And ile be the yong prince, and hit thée a boxe on the eare,
And then thou shalt say, to teach you what prerogatiues
Meane, I commit you to the Fléete.

 Iohn. Come on, Ile be your Iudge,
But thou shalt not hit me hard.

 Der. No, no.

 Iohn. What hath he done?

 Der. Marry he hath robd Dericke.

 Iohn. Why then I cannot let him go.

 Der. I must néeds haue my man.

 Iohn. You shall not haue him.

 Der. Shall I not haue my man, say no and you dare:
How say you, shall I not haue my man?

 Iohn. No marry shall you not.

Der.

Der. Shall I not Iohn?

Iohn. No Dericke.

Der. Why then take you that till moze come,
Sownes, shall I not haue him?

Iohn. Well I am content to take this at your hand,
But I pzay you, who am I?

Der. Who art thou, Sownds, dost not know thy self?

Iohn. No.

Der. Now away simple fellow,
Why man, thou art Iohn the Cobler.

Iohn. No, I am my Lozd chiefe Iustice of England.

Der. Oh Iohn, Masse thou saist true, thou art indeed.

Iohn. Why then to teach you what pzerogatiues mean
I commit you to the Fleete.

Der. Wel I will go, but yfaith you gray beard knaue,

Exit. And straight enters again. (Ile course you.
Oh Iohn, Come, come out of thy chair, why what a clown
weart thou, to let me hit thee a box on the eare, and now
thou seest they will not take me to the Fleete, I thinke that
thou art one of these Wozenday Clownes.

Iohn. But I maruell what will become of thee?

Der. Faith ile be no moze a Carrier.

Iohn. What wilt thou do then?

Der. Ile dwell with thee and be a Cobler.

Iohn. With me, alasse I am not able to keepe thee,
Why thou wilt eate me out of dozres.

Der. Oh Iohn, no Iohn, I am none of these great slou-
ching fellowes, that deuoure these great peeces of beefe and
bzewes, alasse a trifle serues me, a Woodcocke, a Chicken,
oz a Capons legge, oz any such little thing serues me.

Iohn. a Capon, why man, I cannot get a Capon once a
yeare, except it be at Chzistmas, at some other mans house,
foz we Coblers be glad of a dish of rootes.

Der. Rootes, why are you so good at rooting?
Nay Cobler, weele haue you ringde,

Iohn.

Iohn. But Dericke, though we be so poore,
Yet wil we haue in store a crab in the fire,
With nut-browne Ale, that is full stale,
Which wil a man quaile, and laie in the mire.

Der. A bots on you, and be but for your Ale,
Ile dwel with you, come lets away as fast as we can.

Exeunt.

Enter the yoong Prince, with Ned and Tom.

Hen.5. Come away sirs, Gogs wounds Ned,
Didst thou not see what a boxe on the eare
I tooke my Lord chiefe Iustice?

Tom. By gogs blood it did me good to see it,
It made his teeth iarre in his head.

Enter sir Iohn Old-Castle.

Hen.5. How now sir Iohn Old-Castle,
What newes with you?

Ioh.Old. I am glad to see your grace at libertie,
I was come I, to visit you in prison.

Hen.5. To visit me, didst thou not know that I am a
Princes son, why tis inough for me to looke into a prison,
though I come not in my selfe, but heres such adow now a
dayes, heres prisoning, heres hanging, whipping, and the
diuel and all: but I tel you sirs, when I am king, we will
haue no such things, but my lads, if the old king my father
were dead, we would be all kings.

Ioh.Old. Hee is a good olde man, God take him to his
mercy the sooner.

Hen.5. But Ned, so soone as I am king, the first thing
I wil do, shal be to put my Lord chief Iustice out of office,
And thou shalt be my Lord chiefe Iustice of England.

Ned. Shall I be Lord chiefe Iustice?
By gogs wounds, ile be the brauest Lord chiefe Iustice
That euer was in England.

Hen.5. Then Ned, ile turne all these prisons into fence
Schooles, and I will endue thee with them, with landes to

C   main-

maintaine them withall: then I wil haue a bout with my
Lord chiefe Iustice, thou shalt hang none but picke purses
and horse stealers, and such base minded villaines, but that
fellow that will stand by the high way side couragiously
with his sword and buckler and take a purse, that fellow
giue him commendations, beside that, send him to me and
I will giue him an anuall pension out of my Exchequer, to
maintaine him all the dayes of his life.

Ioh. Nobly spoken Harry, we shall neuer haue a mery
world til the old king be dead.

Ned. But whither are ye going now?

Hen. 5. To the Court, for I heare say, my father lies verie sicke.

Tom. But I doubt he wil not die.

Hen. 5. Yet will I goe thither, for the breath shal be no
sooner out of his mouth, but I wil clap the Crowne on my
head.

Iockey. Wil you goe to the Court with that cloake so
full of needles?

Hen. 5. Cloake, ilat-holes, needles, and all was of mine
owne deuising, and therefore I wil weare it.

Tom. I pray you my Lord, what may be the meaning
thereof?

Hen. 5. Why man, tis a signe that I stand vpon thornes,
til the Crowne be on my head.

Ioc. Or that euery needle might be a pricke to their harts
that repine at your doings.

Hen. 5. Thou saist true Iockey, but thers some wil say,
the yong Prince will be a well toward yong man and all
this geare, that I had as leeue they would breake my head
with a pot, as to say any such thing, but we stand prating
here too long, I must needs speake with my father, therfore
come away.

Porter. What a rapping keep you at the Kings Court
gate?

                                                    Hen. 5

Hen.5. Heres one that must speake with the King.

Por. The King is verie sick, and none must speak with him.

Hen.5. No you rascall, do you not know me?

Por. You are my Lord the yong Prince.

Hen.5. Then goe and tell my father, that I must and will speake with him.

Ned. Shall I cut off his head?

Hen.5. No, no, though I would helpe you in other places, yet I haue nothing to do here, what you are in my fathers Court.

Ned. I will write him in my Tables, for so soone as I am made Lord chiefe Iustice, I wil put him out of his Office.

The Trumpet sounds.

Hen.5. Gogs wounds sirs, the King comes, Lets all stand aside.

Enter the King, with the Lord of Exeter.

Hen.4. And is it true my Lord, that my sonne is alreadie sent to the Fleete? now truly that man is more fitter to rule the Realme then I, for by no meanes could I rule my sonne, and he by one word hath caused him to be ruled. Oh my sonne, my sonne, no sooner out of one prison, but into another, I had thought once whiles I had liued, to haue seene this noble Realme of England flourish by thee my sonne, but now I see it goes to ruine and decaie.

He wepeth.

Enters Lord of Oxford.

Ox. And please your grace, here is my Lord your sonne, That commeth to speake with you, He saith, he must and wil speake with you.

Hen.4. Who my sonne Harry?

Oxf. I and please your Maiestie.

Hen.4. I know wherefore he commeth, But looke that none come with him.

C 2 Ox.

The famous victories

Oxf. A verie disordered company, and such as make
Verie ill rule in your Maiesties house.

Hen.4. Well let him come,
But looke that none come with him.

He goeth.

Oxf. And please your grace,
My Lord the king, sends for you.

Hen.5. Come away sirs, lets go all togither.

Oxf. And please your grace, none must go with you.

Hen.5. Why I must needs haue them with me,
Otherwise I can do my father no countenance,
Therefore come away.

Oxf. The king your father commaunds
There should none come.

Hen.5. Well sirs then be gone,
And prouide me three Noyse of Musitians.

Exeunt knights.

Enters the Prince with a dagger in his hand.

Hen.4. Come my sonne, come on a Gods name,
I know wherefore thy comming is,
Oh my sonne, my sonne, what cause hath euer bene,
That thou shouldst forsake me, and follow this vilde and
Reprobate company, which abuseth youth so manifestly:
Oh my sonne, thou knowest that these thy doings
Wil end thy fathers dayes.

He weepes.

I so, so, my sonne, thou fearest not to approach the presence
of thy sick father, in that disguised sort, I tel thee my sonne,
that there is neuer a needle in thy cloke, but it is a prick to
my heart, & neuer an ilat-hole, but it is a hole to my soule:
and wherefore thou bringest that dagger in thy hande I
know not, but by coniecture.

He weepes.

Hen.5. My cōscience accuseth me, most soueraign Lord,
and welbeloued father, to answere first to the last point,
That

That is, whereas you coniecture that this hand and this
dagger shall be armde against your life: no, know my beloued father, far be the thoughts of your sonne, sonne said
I, an vnworthie sonne for so good a father: but farre be the
thoughts of any such pretended mischiefe:and I most humbly render it to your Maiesties hand, and liue my Lord and
soueraigne for euer:and with your dagger arme me show like
vengeance vpon the bodie of that your sonne, I was about
say and dare not, ah woe is me therefore, that your wilde
slaue, tis not the Crowne that I come for, sweete father,
because I am vnworthie,and those vilde & reprobate company I abandon,& vtterly abolish their company for euer.
Pardon sweete father,pardon: the least thing and most de-
sire:and this ruffianly cloake,I here teare from my backe,
and sacrifice it to the diuel,which is maister of al mischiefe:
Pardō me,sweet father,pardon me: good my Lord of Exeter speak for me:pardon me,pardō good father,not a word:
ah he wil not speak one word:A Harry,now thrice vnhappie Harry.But what shal I do? I wil go take me into some
solitarie place, and there lament my sinfull life, and when
I haue done,I wil laie me downe and die.

Exit.

Hen.4. Call him againe,call my sonne againe.
   Hen.5. And doth my father call me again:now Harry,
Happie be the time that thy father calleth thee againe.
   Hen.4. Stand vp my son, and do not think thy father,
But at the request of thee my sonne,I wil pardon thee,
And God blesse thee,and make thee his seruant.
   Hen.5. Thanks good my Lord,& no doubt but this day,
Euen this day,I am borne new againe.
   Hen.4.Come my son and Lords,take me by the hands.

Exeunt omnes.

Enter Dericke.

Der. Thou art a stinking whore, & a whorson stinking
Doest thinke ile take it at thy hands?   (whore,

C 3 Enter

Enter Iohn Cobler running.

Iohn. Derick, D.D.Hearesta,
Do D, neuer while thou liuest vse that,
Why what wil my neighbors say,and thou go away so?

Der. Shees a narrant whore,and Ile haue the lawe on
you Iohn.

Iohn. Why what hath she done?

Der. Marry marke thou Iohn.
I wil proue it that I wil.

Iohn. What wilt thou proue?

Der. That she cald me in to dinner.
Iohn,marke the tale wel Iohn,and when I was set,
She brought me a dish ofrootes,and a peece of barrel butter
therein: and she is a verie knaue,
And thou a drab if thou take her part.

Iohn. Hearesta Dericke,is this the matter?
Nay,and it be no worse,we wil go home againe,
And all shall be amended.

Der. Oh Iohn, hearesta Iohn, is all well?

Iohn. I,all is wel.

Der. Then ile go home before,and breake all the glasse
windowes.

Enter the King with his Lords.

Hen.4. Come my Lords, I see it bootes me not to take
any phisick,for all the Phisitians in the world cannot cure
me,no not one. But good my Lords,remember my last
wil and Testament concerning my sonne, for truly my
Lordes, I do not thinke but he wil proue as valiant and
victorious a King,as euer raigned in England.

Both. Let heauen and earth be witnesse betwéene vs,if
we accomplish not thy wil to the vttermost.

Hen.4. I giue you most vnfained thāks,good my lords,
Draw the Curtaines and depart my chamber a while,
And cause some Musicke to rocke me a sléepe.

He sleepeth. (Exeunt Lords.
Enter

670

680

690

700

22

Enter the Prince.

Hen.5. Ah Harry, thrice vnhappie, that hath neglect so long from visiting of thy sicke father, I wil goe, nay but why do I not go to the Chamber of my sick father, to comfort the melancholy soule of his bodie, his soule said I, here is his bodie indded, but his soule is, whereas it needs no bodie, Now thrice accursed Harry, that hath offended thy father so much, and could not I craue pardon for all. Oh my dying father, curst be the day wherin I was borne, and accursed be the houre wherin I was begotten, but what shal I do: if weeping teares which come too late, may suffice the negligence neglected to some, I wil weepe day and night vntil the fountaine be drie with weeping.

Exit.

Enter Lord of Exeter and Oxford.

Exe. Come easily my Lord, for waking of the king.

Hen.4. Now my Lords.

Oxf. How doth your Grace feele your selfe?

Hen.4. Somewhat better after my slape,
But good my Lords take off my Crowne,
Remoue my chaire a litle backe, and set me right.

Ambo. And please your grace, the crown is take away.

Hen.4. The Crowne taken away,
Good my Lord of Oxford, go see who hath done this deed:
No doubt tis some bilde traitor that hath done it,
To depriue my sonne, they that would do it now,
Would seeke to scrape and scrawle for it after my death.

Enter Lord of Oxford with the Prince.

Oxf. Here and please your Grace,
Is my Lord the yong Prince with the Crowne.

Hen.4. Why how now my sonne?
I had thought the last time I had you in schooling,
I had giuen you a lesson for all,
And do you now begin againe?
Why tel me my sonne,

Doet

Doest thou thinke the time so long,
That thou wouldest haue it before the
Breath be out of my mouth?

Hen.5. Most soueraign Lord, and welbeloued father,
I came into your Chamber to comfort the melancholy
Soule of your bodie, and finding you at that time
Past all recouerie, and dead to my thinking,
God is my witnesse: and what should I do,
But with weeping tears lament ẙ death of you my father,
And after that, seeing the Crowne, I tooke it:
And tel me my father, who might better take it then I,
After your death? but seeing you liue,
I most humbly render it into your Maiesties hands,
And the happiest man aliue, that my father liue:
And liue my Lord and Father, for euer.

Hen.4. Stand vp my sonne,
Thine answers hath sounded wel in mine eares,
For I must need confesse that I was in a very sound sleep,
And altogither vnmindful of thy comming:
But come neare my sonne,
And let me put thee in possession whilst I liue,
That none depriue thee of it after my death.

Hen.5. Well may I take it at your maiesties hands,
But it shal neuer touch my head, so lõg as my father liues.

He taketh the Crowne:

Hen.4. God giue thee ioy my sonne,
God blesse thee and make thee his seruant,
And send thee a prosperous raigne.
For God knowes my sonne, how hardly I came by it,
And how hardly I haue maintained it.

Hen.5. Howsoeuer you came by it, I know not,
But now I haue it from you, and from you I wil keepe it:
And he that seekes to take the Crowne from my head,
Let him looke that his armour be thicker then mine,
Or I will pearce him to the heart,

Were

740

750

760

770

Were it harder then brasse or bollion.

Hen.4. Nobly spoken, and like a king.
Now trust me my Lords, I feare not but my sonne
Will be as warlike and victorious a Prince,
As euer raigned in England.

L. Ambo. His former life shewes no lesse.

Hen.4. wel my lords, I know not whether it be for sleep,
Or drawing neare of drowsie summer of death,
But I am verie much giuen to sleepe,
Therefore good my Lords and my sonne,
Draw the Curtaines, depart my Chamber,
And cause some Musicke to rocke me a sleepe.

Exeunt omnes.

The King dieth.

Enter the Theefe.

Theefe. Ah God, I am now much like to a Bird
Which hath escaped out of the Cage,
For so soone as my Lord chiefe Iustice heard
That the old king was dead, he was glad to let me go,
For feare of my Lord the yong Prince:
But here comes some of his companions,
I wil see and I can get any thing of them,
For old acquaintance.

Enter Knights raunging.

Tom. Gogs wounds, the king is dead.

Ioc. Dead, then gogs blood, we shall be all kings.

Ned. Gogs wounds, I shall be Lord chiefe Iustice
Of England.

Tom. Why how, are you broken out of prison?

Ned. Gogs wounds, how the villaine stinkes.

Ioc. Why what wil become of thee now?
Fie vpon him, how the rascall stinkes.

Theef. Marry I wil go and serue my maister againe.

Tom. Gogs blood, dost think that he wil haue any such
Scab'd knaue as thou art: what man he is a king now.

D   Ned.

Ned. Hold thée, heres a couple of Angels for thée,
And get thée gone, for the King wil not be long
Before he come this way:
And hereafter I wil tel the king of thée.

                                             Exit Theefe. 810

  Ioc. Oh how it did me good, to sée the king
When he was crowned:
Me thought his seate was like the figure of heauen,
And his person like vnto a God.

  Ned. But who would haue thought,
That the king would haue changde his countenance so?

  Ioc. Did you not sée with what grace
He sent his embassage into France, to tel the French ki ng
That Harry of England hath sent for the Crowne,
And Harry of England wil haue it. 820

  Tom. But twas but a litle to make the people b cléene,
That he was sorie for his fathers death.

                           The Trumpet sounds.

  Ned. Gogs wounds, the king comes,
Lets all stand aside.

          Enter the King with the Archbishop, and
              the Lord of Oxford.

  Ioc. How do you my Lord?
  Ned. How now Harry?
Tut my Lord, put away these dumpes, 830
You are a king, and all the realme is yours:
What man, do you not remember the old sayings,
You know I must be Lord chiefe Iustice of England,
Trust me my lord, me thinks you are very much changed,
And tis but with a litle sorrowing, to make folkes beléeue
The death of your father gréeues you,
And tis nothing so.

  Hen.5. I prethée Ned, mend thy maners,
And be more modester in thy tearmes,
For my vnfeined gréefe is not to be ruled by thy flattering 840
                                        And

                        G

And diſſembling talke, thou ſaiſt I am changed,
So I am indæd, and ſo muſt thou be, and that quickly,
Or elſe I muſt cauſe thæ to be chaunged.

Ioc. Gogs wounds how like you this?
Sownds tis not ſo ſwæte as Muſicke.

Tom. I truſt we haue not offended your grace no way.

Hen. 5. Ah Tom, your former life græues me,
And makes me to abandõ & aboliſh your company for euer
And therfore not vpõ pain of death to approch my preſence
By ten miles ſpace, then if I heare wel of you,
It may be I wil do ſomewhat for you,
Otherwiſe looke for no more fauour at my hands,
Then at any other mans: And therefore be gone,
We haue other matters to talke on.

Exeunt Knights.

Now my good Lord Archbiſhop of Canterbury,
What ſay you to our Embaſſage into France?

Archb. Your right to the French Crowne of France,
Came by your great grandmother Izabel,
Wiſe to King Edward the third,
And ſiſter to Charles the French King:
Now if the French king deny it, as likely inough he wil,
Then muſt you take your ſword in hand,
And conquer the right:
Let the vſurped Frenchman know,
Although your predeceſſors haue let it paſſe, you wil not:
For your Country men are willing with purſe and men,
To aide you.
Then my good Lord, as it hath bene alwaies knowne,
That Scotland hath bene in league with France,
By a ſort of penſions which yearly come from thence,
I thinke it therefore beſt to conquere Scotland,
And thē I think that you may go more eaſily into France:
And this is all that I can ſay, My good Lord.   (terbury.

Hen. 5. I thanke you, my good lord Archbiſhop of Can-

D 2   What

What say you my good Lord of Oxford?

Oxf. And And please your Maiestie,
I agrée to my Lord Archbishop, sauing in this,
He that wil Scotland win, must first with France begin:
According to the old saying. (France,
Therefore my good Lord, I thinke it best first to inuade,
For in conquering Scotland, you conquer but one,
And conquere France, and conquere both.

Enter Lord of Exeter.

Exe. And please your Maiestie,
My Lord Embassador is come out of France.

Hen.5. Now trust me my Lord,
He was the last man that we talked of,
I am glad that he is come to resolue vs of our answere,
Commit him to our presence.

Enter Duke of Yorke.

York. God saue the life of my soueraign Lord the king.

Hen.5. Now my good Lord the Duke of Yorke,
What newes from our brother the French king?

Yorke. And please your Maiestie,
I deliuered him my Embassage,
Whereof I toke some deliberation,
But for the answere he hath sent,
My Lord Embassador of Burges, the Duke of Burgony,
Monsieur le Cole, with two hundred and fiftie horsemen,
To bring the Embassage.

Hen.5. Commit my Lord Archbishop of Burges
Into our presence.

Enter Archbishop of Burges.

Now my Lord Archbishop of Burges,
We do learne by our Lord Embassador,
That you haue our message to do
From our brother the French king:
Here my good Lord, according to our accustomed order,
We giue you frée libertie and license to speake,

With

With good audience.

Archb. God saue the mightie king of England,
My Lord and maister, the most Christian king,
Charles the seuenth, the great & mightie king of France,
As a most noble and Christian king,
Not minding to shed innocent blood, is rather content
To yeeld somewhat to your vnreasonable demaunds,
That if fiftie thousand crownes a yeare with his daughter
The said Ladie Katheren, in marriage,
And some crownes which he may wel spare,
Not hurting of his kingdome,
He is content to yeeld so far to your vnreasonable desire.

Hen. 5. Why then belike your Lord and maister,
Thinks to puffe me vp with fifty thousand crowns a yere,
No tell thy Lord and maister,
That all the crownes in France shall not serue me,
Except the Crowne and kingdome it selfe:
And perchance hereafter I wil haue his daughter.

He deliuereth a Tunne of Tennis balles.

Archb. And it please your Maiestie,
My Lord Prince Dolphin greets you well,
With this present.

He deliuereth a Tunne of Tennis Balles.

Hen. 5. What a guilded Tunne?
I pray you my Lord of Yorke, looke what is in it?

Yorke. And it please your Grace,
Here is a Carpet and a Tunne of Tennis balles.

Hen. 5. A Tunne of Tennis balles?
I pray you good my Lord Archbishop,
What might the meaning thereof be?

Archb. And it please you my Lord,
A messenger you know, ought to keepe close his message,
And specially an Embassador.

Hen. 5. But I know that you may declare your message
To a king, the law of Armes allowes no lesse.

D 3   Archb,

Archb. My Lord hearing of your wildnesse before your
Fathers death, sent you this my good Lord,
Meaning that you are more fitter for a Tennis Court
Then a field, and more fitter for a Carpet then the Camp.

Hen.5. My lord prince Dolphin is very pleasant with me: 950
But tel him, that in steed of balles of leather,
We wil tosse him balles of brasse and yron,
Yea such balles as neuer were tost in France,
The proudest Tennis Court shall rue it.
I and thou Prince of Burges shall rue it.
Therfore get thee hence, and tel him thy message quickly,
Least I be there before thee; Away priest, be gone.

Archb. I beseech your grace, to deliuer me your safe
Conduct vnder your broad seale Emanuel.

Hen.5. Priest of Burges, know, 960
That the hand and seale of a King, and his word is all one,
And in stead of my hand and seale,
I will bring him my hand and sword:
And tel thy lord & maister, that I Harry of England said it,
And I Harry of England, wil performe it.
My Lord of Yorke, deliuer him our safe conduct,
Vnder our broad seale Emanuel.

Exeunt Archbishop, and the Duke of Yorke.
Now my Lords, to Armes, to Armes,
For I vow by heauen and earth, that the proudest 970
French man in all France, shall rue the time that euer
These Tennis balles were sent into England.
My Lord, I wil ŷ there be prouided a great Nauy of ships,
With all speed, at South-Hampton,
For there I meane to ship my men,
For I would be there before him, it it were possible,
Therefore come, but staie,
I had almost forgot the chiefest thing of all, with chasing
With this French Embassador.
Call in my Lord chiefe Iustice of England. 980

ε C   Enters

30

Enters Lord chiefe Iustice of England.

Exe. Here is the king my Lord.

Iustice. God preserue your Maiestie.

Hen. 5. Why how now my lord, what is the matter?

Iustice. I would it were vnknowne to your Maiestie.

Hen. 5. Why what aileyou?

Iust. Your Maiestie knoweth my griefe well.

Hen. 5. Oh my Lord, you remember you sent me to the Fléete, did you not?

Iust. I trust your grace haue forgotten that.

Hen. 5. I truly my Lord, and for reuengement,
I haue chosen you to be my Protector ouer my Realme,
Vntil it shall please God to giue me spéedie returne
Out of France.

Iust. And ifit please your Maiestie, I am far vnworthie
Of so high a dignitie.

Hen 5. Tut my Lord, you are not vnworthie,
Because I thinke you worthie:
For you that would not spare me,
I thinke will not spare another,
It must néeds be so, and therefore come,
Let vs be gone, and get our men in a readinesse.

Exeunt omnes.

Enter a Captaine, Iohn Cobler and his wife.

Cap. Come, come, there's no remedie,
Thou must néeds serue the king.

Iohn. Good maister Captaine let me go,
I am not able to goe so farre.

Wife. I pray you good maister Captaine,
Be good to my husband.

Cap. Why I am sure he is not too good to serue ẏ king?

Iohn. Alasse no: but a great deale too bad,
Therefore I pray you let me goe.

Cap. No, no, thou shalt go.

Iohn

Iohn. Oh sir, I haue a great many shooes at home to
Cobble.

Wife. I pray you let him go home againe.

Cap. Tush I care not, thou shalt go.

Iohn. Oh wife, and you had béene a louing wife to me,
This had not bene, for I haue said many times,
That I would go away, and now I must go
Against my will.

                         He weepeth.

         Enters Dericke.

Der. How now ho, *Basillus Manus*, for an old codpéece,
Maister Captaine shall we away?
Sownds how now Iohn, what a crying?
What make you and my dame there?
I maruell whose head you will throw the stooles at,
Now we are gone.

Wife. Ile tell you, come ye cloghead,
What do you with my potlid? heare you,
Will you haue it rapt about your pate?

         She beateth him with her potlid.

Der. Oh god dame, here he shakes her,
And I had my dagger here, I wold worie you al to péeces
That I would.

Wife. Would you so, Ile trie that.

         She beateth him.

Der. Maister Captaine will ye suffer her?
Go too dame, I will go backe as far as I can,
But and you come againe,
Ile clap the law on your backe thats flat:
Ile tell you maister Captaine what you shall do?
Presse her for a souldier, I warrant you,
She will do as much good as her husband and I too.

         Enters the Theefe.

Sownes, who comes yonder?

Cap. How now good fellow, doest thou want a maister?

                      Theefe.

Theefe. I truly sir.

Cap. Hold thee then, I presse thee for a souldier,
To serue the King in France.

Der. How now Gads, what doest knowes thinkest?

Theefe. I, I knew thee long ago.

Der. Heare you maister Captaine?

Cap. What saist thou?

Der. I pray you let me go home againe.

Cap. Why what wouldst thou do at home?

Der. Marry I haue brought two shirts with me,
And I would carry one of them home againe,
For I am sure heele steale it from me,
He is such a filching fellow.

Cap. I warrant thee he wil not steate it from thee,
Come lets away.

Der. Come maister Captaine lets away,
Come follow me.

Iohn. Come wife, lets part louingly.

Wife. Farewell good husband.

Der. Fie what a kissing and crying is here?
Sownes, do ye thinke he wil neuer come againe?
Why Iohn come away, doest thinke that we are so base
Minded to die among French men?
Sownes, we know not whether they will laie
Vs in their Church or no: Come M.Captain, lets away.

Cap. I cannot staie no longer, therefore come away.

Exeunt omnes.

Enter the King, Prince Dolphin, and Lord
high Constable of France.

King. Now my Lord high Constable,
What say you to our Embassage into England?

Const. And it please your Maiestie, I can say nothing,
Vntil my Lords Embassadors be come home,
But yet me thinkes your grace hath done well,
To get your men in so good a readinesse,

C   For

33

For feare of the worst.

King. I my Lord we haue some in a readinesse,
But if the King of England make againſt vs,
We muſt haue thrice so many moe.

Dolphin. Tut my Lord, although the King of England
Be yong and wilde headed, yet neuer thinke he will be so
Vnwise to make battell againſt the mightie king of
France.

King. Oh my sonne, although the King of England be
yong and wilde headed, yet neuer thinke but he is rulde
By his wise Councellors.

      Enter Archbishop of Burges.

Archb. God saue the life of my soueraign lord the king.

King. Now my good Lord Archbishop of Burges,
What newes from our brother the English King?

Archb. And please your Maieſtie,
He is so far from your expectation,
That nothing wil serue him but the Crowne
And kingdome it selfe, besides, he bad me haſte quickly,
Leaſt he be there before me, and so far as I heare,
He hath kept promise, for they say, he is alreadie landed
At Kidcocks in Normandie, vpon the Riuer of Sene,
And laid his siege to the Garrison Towne of Harflew.

King. You haue made great haſte in the meane time,
Haue you not?

Dolphin. I pray you my Lord, how did the King of
England take my presents?

Archb. Truly my Lord, in verie ill part,
For these your balles of leather,
He will toſſe you balles of braſſe and yron:
Truſt me my Lord, I was verie affraide of him,
He is such a hautie and high minded Prince,
He is as fierce as a Lyon.

Con. Tuſh, we wil make him as tame as a Lambe,
I warrant you.

             Enter

Enters a Messenger.

Messen. God saue the mightie King of France.

King. Now Messenger, what newes?

Messen. And it please your Maiestie,

I come from your poore distressed Towne of Harflew,

Which is so beset on euery side,

If your Maiestie do not send present aide,

The Towne will be yeelded to the English King.

King. Come my Lords, come, shall we stand still

Till our Countrey be spoyled vnder our noses?

My Lords, let the Normanes, Brabants, Pickardies,

And Danes, be sent for with all speede:

And you my Lord high Constable, I make Generall

Ouer all my whole Armie.

Monsieur le Colle, Maister of the Boas,

Signior Deuens, and all the rest, at your appointment.

Dolp. I trust your Maiestie will bestow,

Some part of the battell on me,

I hope not to present any otherwise then well.

King. I tell thee my sonne,

Although I should get the victory, and thou lose thy life,

I should thinke my selfe quite conquered,

And the English men to haue the victorie.

Dol. Why my Lord and father,

I would haue the pettie king of England to know,

That I dare encounter him in any ground of the world.

King. I know well my sonne,

But at this time I will haue it thus:

Therefore come away.

Exeunt omnes.

Enters Henry the fifth, with his Lords.

Hen.5. Come my Lords of England,

No doubt this good lucke of winning this Towne,

Is a signe of an honourable victorie to come,

C 2　　　　　　But

But good my Lord, go and speake to the Captaines
With all spéed, to number the hoast of the French men,
And by that meanes we may the better know
How to appoint the battell.

 Yorke. And it please your Maiestie,
There are many of your men sicke and diseased,
And many of them die for want of victuals.

 Hen.5. And why did you not tell me of it before?
If we cannot haue it for money,
We will haue it by dint of sword,
The lawe of Armes allow no lesse.

 Oxf. I beséech your grace, to graunt me a boone.

 Hen.5. What is that my good Lord?

 Oxf. That your grace would giue me the
Euantgard in the battell.

 Hen.5. Trust me my Lord of Oxford, I cannot:
For I haue alreadie giue it to my vncke ye Duke of York,
Yet I thanke you for your good will.

     A Trumpet soundes.
How now, what is that?

 Yorke. I thinke it be some Herald of Armes.
      Enters a Herald.

 Herald. King of England, my Lord high Constable,
And others of the Noble men of France,
Sends me to defie thée, as open enemy to God,
Our Countrey, and vs, and hereupon,
They presently bid thée battell.

 Hen.5. Herald tell them, that I defie them,
As open enemies to God, my Countrey, and me,
And as wronfull vsurpers of my right:
And whereas thou saist they presently bid me battell,
Tell them that I thinke they know how to please me:
But I pray thée what place hath my lord Prince Dolphin
Here in battell.

 Herald. And it please your grace,

          My

My Lord and King his father,
Will not let him come into the field.

Hen.5. Why then he doth me great iniurie,
I thought that he & I shuld haue plaid at tennis togither,
Therefore I haue brought tennis balles for him,
But other maner of ones then he sent me.
And Herald, tell my Lord Prince Dolphin,
That I haue inured my hāds with other kind of weapons
Then tennis balles, ere this time a day,
And that he shall finde it ere it be long,
And so adue my friend:
And tell my Lord, that I am readie when he will.

Exit Herald.

Come my Lords, I care not and I go to our Captaines,
And ile see the number of the French army my selfe.
Strike vp the Drumme.

Exeunt omnes.

Enter French Souldiers.

1. Soul. Come away Jack Drummer, come away all,
And me will tel you what me woil do,
Me woil tro one chance on the dice,
Who shall haue the king of England and his lords.

2. Soul. Come away Jacke Drummer,
And tro your chance, and lay downe your Drumme.

Enter Drummer.

Drum. Oh the braue apparel that the English mans
Hay broth ouer, I wil tel you what
Me ha donue, me ha prouided a hundreth trunkes,
And all to put the fine parel of the English mans in.

1. Soul. What do thou meane by trunkea?

2. Soul. A chest man, a hundred chests.

1. Soul. Awee, awee, awee, Me wil tel you what,
Me ha put fiue shildren out of my house,
And all too litle to put the fine apparel of the
English mans in.

C 3

Drum

37

Drum. Oh the braue, the braue apparel that we shall
Haue anon, but come, and you shall see what me wil tro
At the kings Drummer and Fife,
Ha, me ha no good lucke, tro you.

   3. Sol. Faith me wil tro at ye Earle of Northumberland
And my Lord a Willowby, with his great horse,
Snorting, farting, oh braue horse.

   1. Sol. Ha, bur Ladie you ha reasonable good lucke,
Now I wil tro at the king himselfe,
Ha, me haue no good lucks.

Enters a Captaine.

   Cap. How now what make you here,
So farre from the Campe?

   2. Sol. Shal me tel our captain what we haue done here?
Drum. Awee, awee.

Exeunt Drum, and one Souldier.

   2. Sol. I wil tel you what whe haue doune,
We haue bene troing our chance on the Dice,
But none can win the king.

   Cap. I thinke so, why he is left behind for me,
And I haue set three or foure chaire-makers a worke,
To make a new disguised chaire to set that womanly
king of England in, that all the people may laugh
And scoffe at him.

   2. Soul. Oh braue Captaine.

   Cap. I am glad, and yet with a kinde of pitie
To see the poore king:
Why who euer saw a more flourishing armie in France
In one day, then here is? Are not here all the Peeres of
France? Are not here the Normans with their fierie hand-
Gunnes, and slaunching Curtleaxes?
Are not here the Barbarians with their bard horses,
And lanching speares?
Are not here Pickardes with their Crosbowes & piercing
Dartes,

The

1230

1240

1250

38

The Hennes with their cutting Glaues and sharpe
Carbuckles.

Are not here the Lance knights of Burgondie?
And on the other side, a sute of poore English scabs?
Why take an English man out of his warme bed
And his stale drinke, but one moneth,
And alas what wil become of him?
But giue the Frenchman a Reddish roote,
And he wil liue with it all the dayes of his life.

                                                    Exit.

  2. Soul. Oh the braue apparel that we shall haue of the
English mans.   (Exit.

    Enters the king of England and his Lords.

  Hen.5. Come my Lords and fellowes of armes,
What company is there of the French men?

  Oxf. And it please your Maiestie,
Our Captaines haue numbred them,
And so neare as they can iudge,
They are about threescore thousand horsemen,
And fortie thousand footemen.

  Hen.5. They threescore thousand,
And we but two thousand.
They threescore thousand footemen,
And we twelue thousand.
They are a hundred thousand,
And we fortie thousand, ten to one:
My Lords and louing Country men,
Though we be fewe and they many,
Feare not, your quarrel is good, and God wil defend you:
Plucke vp your hearts, for this day we shall either haue
A valiant victorie, or a honourable death.
Now my Lords, I wil that my vncle the Duke of Yorke,
Haue the auantgard in the battell.
The Earle of Darby, the Earle of Oxford,
The Earle of Kent, the Earle of Nottingham,

                                                    The

The Earle of Huntington, I wil haue beside the army,
That they may come fresh vpon them.
And I my selfe with the Duke of Bedford,
The Duke of Clarence and the Duke of Gloster,
Wil be in the midst of the battell.
Furthermore, I wil that my Lord of Willowby,
And the Earle of Northumberland,
With their troupes of horsmen, be cõtinually running like
Wings on both sides of the army :
My Lord of Northumberland, on the left wing.
Then I wil, that euery archer prouide him a stake of
A tree, and sharpe it at both endes,
And at the first encounter of the horsemen,
To pitch their stakes downe into the ground before them,
That they may gore themselues vpon them,
And then to recoyle backe, and shoote wholly altogither,
And so discomfit them.
Oxf. And it please your Maiestie,
I wil take that in charge, if your grace be therwith côtent.
Hen. With all my heart, my good Lord of Oxford:
And go and prouide quickly.
Oxf. I thanke your highnesse.

Exit.

Hen.5. Well my Lords, our battels are ordeined,
And the French making of bonfires, and at their bankets,
But let them looke, for I meane to set vpon them.

The Trumpet soundes.

Soft, heres comes some other French message.

Enters Herauld.

Herald. King of England, my Lord high Constable,
And other of my Lords, considering the poore estate of thée
And thy poore Countrey men,
Sends me to know what thou wilt giue for thy ransome?
Perhaps thou maist agrée better cheape now,
Then when thou art conquered.

Hen.5.

Hen.5. Why then belike your high Constable,
Sends to know what I wil giue for my ransome?
Now trust me Herald, not so much as a tun of tennis bals
No not so much as one poore tennis ball,
Rather shall my bodie lie dead in the field, to feed crowes,
Then euer England shall pay one penny ransome
For my bodie.

Herald. A kingly resolution.

Hen.5. No Herald, tis a kingly resolution,
And the resolution of a king:
Here take this for thy paines.

                                        Exit Herald.

But stay my Lords, what time is it?

All. Prime my Lord.

Hen.5. Then is it good time no doubt,
For all England praieth for vs:
What my Lords, me thinks you looke cheerfully vpon me?
Why then with one voice and like true English hearts,
With me throw vp your caps, and for England,
Cry S. George, and God and S. George helpe vs.
        Strike Drummer.   Exeunt omnes.

The French men crie within, S. Dennis, S. Dennis,
                Mount Ioy S. Dennis.
                The Battell.
        Enters King of England, and his Lords.

Hen.5. Come my Lords come, by this time our
Swords are almost drunke with French blood,
But my Lords, which of you can tell me how many of our
Army be slaine in the battell?

Oxf. And it please your Maiestie,
There are of the French armie slaine,
Aboue ten thousand, twentie sixe hundred,
Whereof are Princes and Nobles bearing banners:
Besides, all the Nobilitie of France are taken prisoners.

                F   Of.

Of your Maiesties Armie, are slaine none but the good
Duke of Yorke, and not aboue fiue or sir and twentie
Common souldiers.

Hen. 5. For the good Duke of Yorke my vnckle,
I am heartily sorie, and greatly lament his misfortune,
Yet the honourable victorie which the Lord hath giuen vs,
Doth make me much reioyce. But state,
Here comes another French message.

Sound Trumpet.

Enters a Herald and kneeleth.

Her. God saue the life of the most mightie Conqueror,
The honourable king of England.

Hen. 5. Now Herald, me thinks the world is changed
With you now, what I am sure it is a great disgrace for a
Herald to knéele to the king of England,
What is thy message?

Her. My Lord & maister, the conquered king of France,
Sends thée long health, with heartie gréeting.

Hen. 5. Herald, his gréetings are welcome,
But I thanke God for my health:
Well Herald, say on.

Herald. He hath sent me to desire your Maiestie,
To giue him leaue to go into the field to view his poore
Country men, that they may all be honourably buried.

Hen. 5. Why Herald, doth thy Lord and maister
Send to me to burie the dead?
Let him bury them a Gods name.
But I pray thée Herald, where is my Lord hie Constable,
And those that would haue had my ransome?

Herald. And it please your maiestie,
He was slaine in the battell.

Hen. 5. Why you may sée, you will make your selues
Sure before the victorie be wonne, but Herald,
What Castle is this so néere adioyning to our Campe?

Herald. And it please your Maiestie,

Tis

1370

1380

1390

Tis cald the Castle of Agincourt.

Hen. 5. Well then my lords of England,
For the more honour of our English men,
I will that this be for euer cald the battell of Agincourt.

Herald. And it please your Maiestie,
I haue a further message to deliuer to your Maiestie.

Hen. 5. What is that Herald? say on.

Her. And it please your Maiestie, my Lord and maister,
Craues to parley with your Maiestie.

Hen. 5. With a good will, so some of my Nobles
View the place for feare of trecherie and treason.

Herald. Your grace néeds not to doubt that.

         Exit Herald.

Hen. 5. Well, tell him then, I will come.
Now my lords, I will go into the field my selfe,
To view my Country men, and to haue them honourably
Buried, for the French king shall neuer surpasse me in
Curtesie, whiles I am Harry king of England.
Come on my lords.

         Exeunt omnes.

    Enters Iohn Cobler, and Robbin Pewterer.

Robin. Now, Iohn Cobler,
Didst thou sée how the king did behaue himselfe?

Iohn. But Robin, didst thou sée what a pollicie
The king had, to sée how the French men were kild
With the stakes of the trées.

Robin. I Iohn, there was a braue pollicie.

    Enters an English souldier, roming.

Soul. What are you my maisters?

Both. Why we be English men.

Soul. Are you English men, then change your language
For the kings Tents are set a fire,
And all they that speake English will be kild.

Iohn. What shall we do Robin? faith ile shift,
For I can speake broken French.

      F 2   Robin.

Robin. Faith so can J,lets heare how thou canst speak?

Iohn. Commodeuales Monsieur.

Robin. Thats well,come lets be gone.

Drum and Trumpet sounds:

Enters Dericke roming. After him a Frenchman,
and takes him prisoner.

Dericke. O good Mounser.

French man. Come,come,you villeaco. 1440

Der. O J will sir, J will.

Frenchman. Come quickly you pesant.

Der. J will sir,what shall J giue you?

French. Marry thou shalt giue me,

One,to,tre,foure,hundred Crownes.

Der. Nay sir, J will giue you more,

J will giue you as many crowns as wil lie on your sword.

French. Wilt thou giue me as many crowns

As will lie on my sword? 1450

Der. J marrie will J, J but you must lay downe your

Sword,or else they will not lie on your sword.

Here the Frenchman laies downe his sword,and
the clowne takes it vp,and hurles him downe.

Der. Thou villaine,darest thou looke vp?

French. O good Mounsier comparteue.

Monsieur pardon me.

Der. O you villaine,now you lie at my mercie,

Doest thou remember since thou lambst me in thy short els 1460

O villaine,now J will strike off thy head.

Here whiles he turnes his backe,the French
man runnes his wayes.

Der. What is he gone,masse J am glad of it,

For if he had staid, J was afraid he wold haue sturd again,

And then J should haue béene spilt,

But J will away,to kill more Frenchmen.

Enters King of France,King of England,
and attendants.

Hen.5.

Hen.5. Now my good brother of France,
My comming into this land was not to shead blood,
But for the right of my Countrey, which if you can deny,
I am content peaceably to leaue my siege,
And to depart out of your land.

Charles. What is it you demand,
My louing brother of England?

Hen.5. My Secretary hath it written, read it.

Secretary. Item, that immediately Henry of England
Be crowned King of France.

Charles. A very hard sentence,
My good brother of England.

Hen. 5. No more but right, my good brother of France.

French King. Well read on.

Secret. Item, that after the death of the said Henry,
The Crowne remaine to him and his heires for euer.

French King. Why then you do not onely meane to
Dispossesse me, but also my sonne.

Hen. 5. Why my good brother of France,
You haue had it long inough :
And as for Prince Dolphin,
It skils not though he sit beside the saddle :
Thus I haue set it downe, and thus it shall be.

French King. You are very peremptorie,
My good brother of England.

Hen. And you as peruerse, my good brother of France.

Charles. Why then belike, all that I haue here is yours.

Hen.5. I euen as far as the kingdom of France reaches

Charles. I for by this hote beginning,
We shall scarce bring it to a calme ending.

Hen.5. It is as you please, here is my resolution.

Charles. Well my brother of England,
If you will giue me a coppie,
We will meete you againe to morrow.

       Exit King of France, and all their attendants.

F 3   Hen.5.

45

Hen.5. With a good will my good brother of France.
Secretary deliuer him a coppie.
My lords of England go before,
And I will follow you.　　　　　　　　Exeunt Lords.
　　　　　　　Speakes to himselfe.
Hen.5. Ah Harry, thrice vnhappie Harry.
Hast thou now conquered the French King,
And begins a fresh supply with his daughter,
But with what face canst thou seeke to gaine her loue,
Which hath sought to win her fathers Crowne?
Her fathers Crowne said I, no it is mine owne:
I but I loue her, and must craue her,
Nay I loue her and will haue her.
　　　　　Enters Lady Katheren and her Ladies.
But here she comes:
How now faire Ladie, Katheren of France,
What newes?
　Kathren. And it please your Maiestie,
My father sent me to know if you will debate any of these
Vnreasonable demands which you require:
　Hen.5. Now trust me Kate,
I commend thy fathers wit greatly in this,
For none in the world could sooner haue made me debate it
If it were possible:
But tell me sweete Kate, canst thou tell how to loue?
　Kate. I cannot hate my good Lord,
Therefore far vnfit were it for me to loue.
　Hen.5. Tush Kate, but tell me in plaine termes,
Canst thou loue the King of England?
I cannot do as these Countries do,
That spend halfe their time in woing:
Tush wench, I am none such,
But wilt thou go ouer to England?
　Kate. I would to God, that I had your Maiestie,
As fast in loue, as you haue my father in warres,

　　　　　　　　　　　　　　　　　　　I

1510

1520

1530

46

I would not vouchsafe so much as one looke,
Untill you had related all these vnreasonable demands.

Hen.5. Tush Kate, I know thou wouldst not vse me so
Hardly: But tell me, canst thou loue the king of England?

Kate. How should I loue him, that hath dealt so hardly
With my father.

Hen.5. But ile deale as easily with thée,
As thy heart can imagine, or tongue can require,
How saist thou, what will it be?

Kate. If I were of my owne direction,
I could giue you answere:
But seeing I stand at my fathers direction,
I must first know his will.

Hen.5. But shal I haue thy good wil in the mean season?

Kate. Whereas I can put your grace in no assurance,
I would be loth to put you in any dispaire.

Hen.5. Now before God, it is a swéete wench.
She goes aside, and speakes as followeth.

Kat. I may thinke my selfe the happiest in the world,
That is beloued of the mightie king of England.

Hen.5. Well Kate, are you at hoast with me?
Swéete Kate, tel thy father from me,
That none in the world could soner haue perswaded me to
It then thou, and so tel thy father from me.

Kat. God kéepe your Maiestie in good health.
Exit. Kat.

Hen.5. Farwel swéet Kate, in faith, it is a swéet wench,
But if I knew I could not haue her fathers good wil,
I would so rowse the Towers ouer his eares,
That I would make him be glad to bring her me,
Upon his hands and knées.
Exit King.

Enters Dericke, with his girdle full of shooes.
Der. How now? Sownes it did me good to sée how
I did triumph ouer the French men.
Enters

The famous victories

Enters Iohn Cobler rouing, with a packe full
of apparell.

Iohn. Whoope Dericke, how doest thou?

Der. What Iohn, Comedeuales, aliue yet.

Iohn. I promise thée Dericke, I scapte hardly,
For I was within halfe a mile when one was kild.

Der. Were you so?

Iohn. I trust me, I had like bene slaine.

Der. But once kild, why it tis nothing,
I was foure or fiue times slaine.

Iohn. Foure or fiue times slaine.
Why how couldst thou haue béene aliue now?

Der. O Iohn, neuer say so,
For I was cald the bloodie souldier amongst them all.

Iohn. Why what didst thou?

Der. Why I will tell thée Iohn,
Euery day when I went into the field,
I would take a straw and thrust it into my nose,
And make my nose bléed, and then I wold go into the field,
And when the Captaine saw me, he would say,
Peace a bloodie souldier, and bid me stand aside,
Whereof I was glad:
But marke the chance Iohn.
I went and stood behinde a trée, but marke then Iohn.
I thought I had béene safe, but on a sodaine,
There steps to me a lustie tall French man,
Now he drew, and I drew,
Now I lay here, and he lay there,
Now I set this leg before, and turned this backward,
And skipped quite ouer a hedge,
And he saw me no more there that day,
And was not this well done Iohn?

Iohn. Masse Dericke, thou hast a wittie head.

Der. I Iohn, thou maist sée, if thou hadst také my cousel,
But what hast thou there?

I thinke

48

I thinke thou haſt bene robbing the French men.

Iohn. I faith Dericke, I haue gotten ſome reparrell
To carry home to my wife.

Der. And I haue got ſome ſhoes,
For ile tel thee what I did, when they were dead,
I would go take off all their ſhoes.

Iohn. I but Dericke, how ſhall we get home?

Der. Nay ſownds, and they take thee,
They wil hang thee,
O Iohn, neuer do ſo, if it be thy fortune to be hangd,
Be hangd in thy owne language whatſoeuer thou doeſt.

Iohn. Why Dericke the warres is done,
We may go home now.

Der. I but you may not go before you aſke the king leaue,
But I know a way to go home, and aſke the king no leaue.

Iohn. How is that Dericke?

Der. Why Iohn, thou knoweſt the Duke of Yorkes
Funerall muſt be carried into England, doeſt thou not?

Iohn. I that I do.

Der. Why then thou knoweſt weele go with it.

Iohn. I but Dericke, how ſhall we do for to meet them?

Der. Sownds if I make not ſhift to meet them, hang me.
Sirra, thou knowſt that in euery Towne there wil
Be ringing, and there wil be cakes and drinke,
Now I wil go to the Clarke and Sexton
And keepe a talking, and ſay, O this fellow rings well,
And thou ſhalt go and take a peece of cake, then ile ring,
And thou ſhalt ſay, oh this fellow keepes a good ſtint,
And then I will go drinke to thee all the way:
But I maruel what my dame wil ſay when we come home,
Becauſe we haue not a French word to caſt at a Dog
By the way?

Iohn. Why what ſhall we do Dericke?

Der. Why Iohn, ile go before and call my dame whore,
And thou ſhalt come after and ſet fire on the houſe,

G   We

We may do it Iohn, for ile proue it,
Because we be souldiers.

The Trumpets sound.

Iohn. Dericke helpe me to carry my shoes and bootes.

Enters King of England, Lord of Oxford and Exeter, then
    the King of France, Prince Dolphin, and the Duke of
    Burgondie, and attendants.

Hen.5. Now my good brother of France,
I hope by this time you haue deliberated of your answere?   1650
  Fr.King. I my welbeloued brother of England,
We haue biewed it ouer with our learned Councell,
But cannot finde that you should be crowned
King of France.
  Hen.5. What not King of France, then nothing,
I must be King : but my louing brother of France,
I can hardly forget the late iniuries offered me,
When I came last to parley,
The French men had better a raked   1660
The bowels out of their fathers carkasses,
Then to haue fiered my Tentes,
And if I knew thy sonne Prince Dolphin for one,
I would so rowse him, as he was neuer so rowsed.
  Fr.King. I dare sweare for my sonnes innocencie
In this matter.
But if this please you, that immediately you be
Proclaimed and crowned heire and Regent of France,
Not King, because I my selfe was once crowned King.
  Hen.5. Heire and Regent of France, that is well,   1670
But that is not all that I must haue.
  Fr.King. The rest my Secretary hath in writing.
  Secret. Item, that Henry King of England,
Be Crowned heire and Regent of France,
During the life of King Charles, and after his death,

The

The Crowne with all rights, to remaine to King Henry
Of England, and to his heires for euer.

    Hen.5. Well my good brother of France,
There is one thing I must needs desire.

    Fr.King. What is that my good brother of England?

    Hen.5. That all your Nobles must be sworne to be true
    to me.

    Fr.King. Whereas they haue not stucke with greater
Matters, I know they wil not sticke with such a trifle,
Begin you my Lord Duke of Burgondie.

    Hen.5. Come my Lord of Burgondie,
Take your oath vpon my sword.

    Burgon. I Philip Duke of Burgondie,
Sweare to Henry king of England,
To be true to him, and to become his league-man,
And that if I Philip, heare of any forraigne power
Comming to inuade the said Henry or his heires,
Then I the said Philip to send him word,
And aide him with all the power I can make,
And thereunto I take my oath.

                              He kisseth the sword.

    Hen.5. Come Prince Dolphin, you must sweare too.

                              He kisseth the sword.

    Hen.5. Well my brother of France,
There is one thing more I must needs require of you.

    Fr.King. Wherein is it that we may satisfie your

    Hen.5. A trifle my good brother of France.   (Maiestie?
I meane to make your daughter Queene of England,
If she be willing, and you therewith content:
How saist thou Kate, canst thou loue the King of England?

    Kate. How should I loue thee, which is my fathers enemy?

    Hen.5. Tut stand not vpon these points,
Tis you must make vs friends:
I know Kate, thou art not a litle proud, that I loue thee:
What wench, the King of England?

                                   French

The famous victories

French King. Daughter let nothing stand betwixt the King of England and thée, agrée to it.

Kate. I had best whilst he is willing, Least when I would, he will not: I rest at your Maiesties commaund.

Hen.5. Welcome swéet Kate, but my brother of France, What say you to it?

French king. With all my heart I like it, But when shall be your wedding day?

Hen.5. The first Sunday of the next moneth, God willing.

Sound Trumpets.

Exeunt omnes.

FINIS.